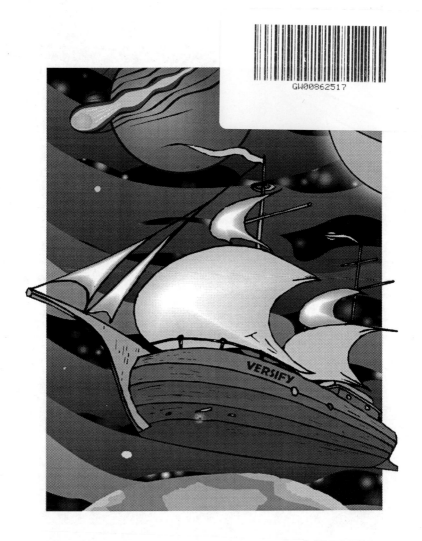

POETIC VOYAGES NORWICH

Edited by Dave Thomas

First published in Great Britain in 2002 by
YOUNG WRITERS
Remus House,
Coltsfoot Drive,
Peterborough, PE2 9JX
Telephone (01733) 890066

HB ISBN 0 75433 410 4
SB ISBN 0 75433 411 2

FOREWORD

Young Writers was established in 1991 with the aim to promote creative writing in children, to make reading and writing poetry fun.

This year once again, proved to be a tremendous success with over 88,000 entries received nationwide.

The Poetic Voyages competition has shown us the high standard of work and effort that children are capable of today. It is a reflection of the teaching skills in schools, the enthusiasm and creativity they have injected into their pupils shines clearly within this anthology.

The task of selecting poems was therefore a difficult one but nevertheless, an enjoyable experience. We hope you are as pleased with the final selection in *Poetic Voyages Norwich* as we are.

CONTENTS

Bawburgh CP School

William Lee	68
Ben Radford	68
Holly Topsom	69
Nathan Shreeve Smith & Nicholas French	69
Victoria Ragan	70
Nadia O'Brien	70
Stacey Gibb	71

Great Witchingham VA Primary School

Trystan Watts	71
Miles Robertson	72
William Powles	72
Vita Sunter	73
Lucy Bower	73
Sarah Burton	74
Katie Symonds	74
Faye Walker	75

Gresham Village School

Joshua Walker	75
Jessica Kerr	75
Natasha Lloyd	76
Thomas Britton	76
Debbie Holt	77
Kerry Kinsley	78
Deborah Wrighton	79
Samantha Bayle	80
Sophie Cowper Johnson	81

Neatishead VC Primary School

Christopher Barlow	81
Lauren Simpson	82
Dominic McIntyre	82
Lewis Clinch	83
Stephanie Culling	83

Notre Dame Preparatory School

Nicola Shattock	84

Emily Ticehurst	84
Nathan Goose	85
Francesca Stafford-Pelham	86
Nicole Oakley	86
Amy Holmwood	87
Abigail Baxter	87
Alexander Kelly	88
Amelia Cheeseman	88
Katrina Chia	89
Joseph Malpas	90
Maxwell Higgins	90
Jenna Slaughter	91
Bryony Stanley	92
Edward McNally	92
Harriet Steggles	93
Lucinda Steggles	93
Harry Millbank	94
Emily Baxter	95
Bethany Richards	95
Emma Lusher	96
Meike Yallop	96
Georgia Levell	97
Hollie Carter	98
Chloe Bulpett	98
Rosie Thomas	99
Samuel Tawn	99
Rebecca Thouless	100
Sabrina Johnson	100
Matthew Adlard	101
Matilda Fitzmaurice	101
Roxanne Mitchell	102
Harriet Kefford	102

St Mary's VC Middle School, Long Stratton

Emma Rust	103
Emma Helliwell	103
Christopher Bartram	104
Samantha Jackson	104

Wensum Middle School

Woodland View Middle School

Elizabeth Dewsbury	199
Kerry-Louise Locke	200
Rosina Webb	200
Tanya Sadd	201
James Beck	202
Kimberley Rowe	202
Gina Atherton	203
Sean Farrow	204
Jonathan Brockett	204
Laura Dawson	205
Thomas Field	206
Emmaleigh Webb	207
Hannah Mayes	208
Peter Berryman	208
Hannah Watson	209
Emma Cooper	210
Laura Parker	210
Abbi Finney	211
Charlotte Morgan	212
Emma Johnson	212
Benji Moon	213
Emma Wilcock	214
Matthew Plane	214
Karl Curson	215
Ben Williams	216
Katie Burns	216
Sam Davison	217
Nathan Glenton	218
Holly Goodrum	218
Charlotte Last	219
Jordan Hare	219
Chelsie Riley	220
Siobhan Allen	220
John Taylor	221
Luke Goffin	222
Jasmine Palmer	223
Evie Warren	224
Adam White	224

The Poems

ELEPHANT

Elephant began.
She took the heaviness of a huge boulder,
She took the loudness of a thunderstorm,
She took the thumping of a volcano
And made her feet.

For her body
She took the wrinkles of an old man,
She took the roughness of a sandpaper block,
She took the power of deadly poison.

From heavy rocks
She took the piercing noise of a tremendous scream,
She took the movement of rolling waves
For her walk.

Then at night
Elephant took the brightness of a shooting star,
She took the sadness of a dead body
To make her eyes.

Movement and ability
Went in the adjustment of her trunk
And for its shape
She took a roughened tree trunk.

And Elephant was made.

Olivia Sewell (11)

THE SLEEPER

After limping the long march,
and crawling while the rest limped;
He lay against his pack while
his astral image fell into darkness.

In the swirling nothing of his dreams
he leapt: as if electricity coursed through
his bones. The limbs then again slackened:
into a shortened sleep.

The leaden pill that had intruded
drew slow red wine as if ruled
by a transparent inch-stick. The blood
seeped into a sea of khaki.

Time passed and still he sleeps:
laying without luxury in a cold stone tomb,
or otherwise just under - shunted down
by endless rain into the crumbling earth.

Who knows? Who cares? Only the shrapnel-cloud
saw the name printed on his identity disc,
lost forever in the swirling mists of time.

Natalie Lewendon (11)
Angel Road Middle School

MY LITTLE SISTER

My little sister is so funny
She's sweet and dear
I love her very much
In my own special way.

She makes me laugh as she giggles
And plays turning my home upside down.
But she's my little sister
And my friend for always.

Bianca Vincent (9)
Angel Road Middle School

I LIKE SCHOOL!

School is educational
My favourite thing's PE
I quite like maths but not as much
I really hate RE.

The summer term is groovy
I love to see the sun
I wish break time could last all day
But nothing would get done.

The winter's bleak and boring
Because it's really cold
Don't run in the corridor
We're always being told.

I like doing my homework
I want to get it right
A half an hour's work
Can sometimes take all night.

I really like my teacher
And the others too
They always laugh and joke with me
When I'm feeling blue.

Stevie-Marie Curtis (10)
Angel Road Middle School

WINTER DAYS

When the snow falls and it turns to ice.
Leaves get stood on, green, yellow and red.
When the trees look dead but they are not.
Branches break, leaves fall off.
Robins sing squeak, squeak, squeak.
Flowers get snowy.
Everything turns to ice.
Scarves, gloves, hats, you need them all.
When your cheeks get cold and red.

Amy Wilde (8)
Angel Road Middle School

NIKKI

A nice little girlie called Nikki,
Found riding a bike very tricky.
She didn't get far,
Before she fell off in some tar
And ended up all hot and sticky.

Oliver David Emes-Ellis (11)
Angel Road Middle School

HOMEWORK POEM

The day I get my homework
I do it straight away
I put it in my bag
Then I put it in my tray.

Latoya Louise Clarke (9)
Angel Road Middle School

SUMMER

The pansies are colourful,
The roses are bright,
The petunias are beautiful,
The daisies are a sight,
The water lilies are pretty,
The Mrs's breakfast is a delight,
All on a warm summer's morning.

The cats are catching,
The blue tits are flying,
The rabbits are digging,
The gardeners are sighing,
The birds are pecking,
The Mrs is lying,
All on a hot summer's day.

As everything lies down to rest,
The pond is still,
The slight breeze rattles in the trees,
Everything's stopped at the mill,
Water dribbles out of the fountain,
The Mrs leans out onto the window sill,
All as the sun sets on a summer's evening.

The ball of fire has disappeared,
Now the stars light up the sky,
The moon shines brightly,
Wispy clouds float by,
Mr Jones sits down to supper
And the Mrs serves up her apple pie,
All on a cool summer's night.

Maria Glew (9)
Angel Road Middle School

FIREWORKS

Fireworks, fireworks shooting in the sky
The prettiest colours flying by
People gasp - the rockets are so fast
The best usually kept till last
Children watch all the bright sparkles
Glowing pretty and bright in the darkness
The children's faces have big smiles
The fireworks really can glow for a mile
And then when you hear the loudest boom
It is usually time for all to go home.

Christina Jessop (10)
Angel Road Middle School

A RAINBOW

I am beautiful, beautiful and bright.
I appear when sun and rain are near,
I have all the colours you can think of,
Red, yellow, pink and green, orange, purple and blue.
But I am upset because I only come out,
When sun and rain are here.
No one can find the surprise at my end,
Everyone's jealous of me and how I am,
But no one can see me in the night.
Not everyone can see me in the day.
But when they do I am so, so, so bright.

Jenna Leeds (11)
Angel Road Middle School

THE PLAYGROUND RAP

Down in the playground,
comin' out the door,
is the cool one causin' uproar.

He goes through the dinner door,
lookin' quite proud,
shoutin' like a maniac bein' very loud.

Has his lunch,
all alone,
very lonely, wants to go home.

Back in the playground,
playin' loads of games,
gettin' lots of attention speedy as flames.

Robert Wilde (10)
Angel Road Middle School

GROOVY CHICK

Girls in a gang with the latest fashions
Girls with rock passions
Girls with electric guitars
Girls with red sports cars
Girls who are big pop stars
Who's the groovy chicks?
    We are!

Jenna Laura Greenacre (10)
Angel Road Middle School

ANIMALS

Sharks
Sharks are fast and nasty
Can be very large and wet
Sharks are my favourite animals
But I have not met one yet.

Cats
Cats can be large and nasty
But can also be small and fluffy
Cats are furry meat-eaters
My cat is fat and stuffy.

Birds
Birds are feathery, dry animals
Can be large and also small
Some are nasty meat-eaters
Some can be pretty and colourful.

Snails
Snails are small and live in a shell
They can be wet and also dry
They return to their shell when I pass by
For snails are slow and shy.

Mouse
Always running from the cat
A mouse's home is in the wall
Mice eat cheese and scraps of food
A mouse is fast but very small.

Snake
Snakes eat meat, usually eggs
Snakes can be dry and some can be wet
They're very fast, large and scary
I use to have one as a pet.

Rosie McKee (11)
Avenue Middle School

THE ENVELOPE

I have an envelope,
I think it's really cool.
I'd better put it down now,
It's time to go to school.
My cat sits on a mat looking at it,
Then she takes it to her den,
Then it's taken by a wren.
The wren lands on the ground,
Then it's taken by a hound.
The hound runs far out of reach,
Till he's at the beach.
The envelope flies into a tree,
Then it falls into the sea.
Splosh, splish,
It's taken by a fish.
The fish twirls and curls,
Then it sees me in my frock.
The envelope lands on a rock.
Although it's very soggy,
Who's to find it but my little doggy.
He comes and drops it on my lap,
I open it - it's . . . it's . . . it's a map!
I get up and start to roam
But look, it's time to go home.
I look all around the house,
I even looked under a toy mouse.
It's no good, I will never find it now
But wait - what's under my dog's collar?
Yahoo! It's a golden dollar.
My sister's given me another envelope.

Olivia Howard (8)
Avenue Middle School

WORMS

This is what some people think of worms:
They think they're disgusting, are slimy, have germs.
But alas they are wrong, so hop aboard,
Come along, to see what worms really are.
Some worms are clever, some worms are cool,
Some worms are helpful, some worms eat gruel!
Some worms are fat, some are slim,
Some worms are gentle,
Some worms drink gin!
Most worms like parties but some worms are quiet,
Some worms are crazy and love to have a riot!
So now you know what worms really are,
Please try to understand that in every worm there is a star.

Anna Fay Horton (9)
Avenue Middle School

THE DREAM

The air was silent
The sky was black
Even the most fearless warriors
Would have travelled back
But I carried on through
The wind and rain
But then I sat it, fall and fearsome
Eyes like fire
Jaws like knives.
Then I woke up, safe in my bed
And it was all just a dream
Or so the storytellers tell.

Ben Allen (8)
Avenue Middle School

COMPUTERS

I like ICT, I enjoy playing on the keys,
The mouse goes up and down and round and round,
At a click of a button you get the sound.

Press the keys one, two, three,
Then you can learn the ABC,
From left to right you can find any subject on your mind.

You can print, you can scan,
Learn lots with just one hand.

You can have fun on your computer,
On your own or with a tutor.

Nicole Reynolds (8)
Avenue Middle School

THE MOON

Moon, moon in the night sky so bright
With your stolen sunlight
When the Earth gets between you two
It makes night vision hard to view

Your rough texture
Your craters too
At night it looks over you

I'm so glad to be able to
Look up at you . . .

Ricky Hawkins (9)
Avenue Middle School

NICKNAMES

My name is often Gypsy Joe,
But others call me Tim.
My best friend's name is sometimes John,
But usually it's Jim.
There's my brother, Stinky Poo,
Though really it is Greg.
And of course my sister, Mood Dude,
Though her friends just call her Meg.
My mum and dad, I know, of course, it must be Hug and Kiss,
But to ruin our fun it had to be boring Jo and Chris.
The twins that live just down the road, we call them Double Act,
But really it is Bill and Bob, we know that for a fact.
Then there's Melissa, Beauty Queen in her lovely silken gown,
And every boy she passes just stops and kneels right down.

I wish I knew just all the names and nicknames I must add,
Of all the children on this Earth and label them with tags.
Oh wouldn't it be lovely to name most every child,
And just say 'Hi' when they walked past and give a great big *smile!*

Hannah Tigerschiold (10)
Avenue Middle School

MY DAD

My dad, he isn't so bad
Most people say he is kind of mad
But to me he is just my dad
So all those people must be mad
I think my dad is number one
And those who don't must be dumb
He is the best of the best
He is much better than all the rest.

Jordan Copland (8)
Avenue Middle School

My Hats

I have many hats
All shapes and sizes
Colours, from back to white,
Spectacular colours to see,
But still warm and snug.

First I have a the Gnome hat,
Red, tall, bendy like a Gnome's hat.
It can be worn in two ways,
Pulled straight down your face,
Or rested high on your head.

Then you have the Rainbow hat,
All the colours of the Rainbow:
Red, blue, green, yellow, orange
And many more colours too,
Just like an actor's hat, sort of.

Last but not least, though still first,
Number one, the GWI hat, yes;
The one and only, the get with it hat
Also known as turnip head.
Whether big or small, colourful, I like them all.

Ben Paul (10)
Avenue Middle School

Art! Art!

Art is fun and messy.
I like art because you get to paint and make a mess.
You can use bright colours and different materials.
So that is why art is my favourite subject.

Yusra Labead (9)
Avenue Middle School

The Thing In The Dark

I'm sitting here,
In the dark,
On my own,
In the middle of a black room.
On each side, I see nothing,
Nothing at all!
From the darkness I noticed:
A wild yellow eye.
Two,
Three,
Four,
And then:

Rar, rar, rar!

Martha Baulcombe (10)
Avenue Middle School

The Waterfall

That waterfall
It sploshed and splashed

Drips off rocks
Gushes down
To that bottomless pit

Drizzles and dribbles
Trickles and streams

It's just a waterfall

Rachel Durrant (8)
Avenue Middle School

I ONCE MET A LADY FROM . . .

I once met a lady from Norwich,
Who couldn't stop eating porridge;
She grew very fat,
Till she couldn't feed her cat,
So she went on a diet from porridge.

I once met a lady from Leeds,
Who had a garden full of weeds;
She dug them all up,
And put them in a cup,
So that she could drink all her weeds.

I once met a lady from Wales,
Who couldn't stop telling tales;
A policeman once came,
And put her in pain,
So that was the end of her tales.

I once met a lady from Aberdeen,
Who always was very clean;
She stood in a puddle,
For she was in a muddle,
Till she never again was clean.

I once met a lady from Consett,
Who had a brand new phone set;
She used it all day,
Till she had a large bill to pay,
So to pay, she had to sell her phone set.

Rachel Varley (9)
Avenue Middle School

A Warm Winter Bed

I just want to stay in bed,
'Cos out there I've got loads to dread.
It's freezing, its cold,
That's what I've been told.
I get up and look outside,
And there the snow lied.
All crispy and white,
The most beautiful sight.
All except the road,
You should see all that grit, there's loads.
The lorries have been,
Hey there's Dean,
And Sooze,
Who hates to lose,
All the games and fights.
Sometimes she likes to use the deadly bites.
The time is ticking,
All the snow is sticking.
The Christmas dinner is nearly here,
There's my dad, he's getting the beer.
I'm so glad school is over,
But I want to see my nan, she lives in Dover.
'Come and get it,' my parents shout,
'Dinner's ready, well just about.'
It smells so good,
I went in to find Sarah watching Robin Hood.
Look, look my nan is here,
She's drinking my dad's whiskey and beer.
Er - Uncle Paul showed us our little cousin's nasty nappy.
Oh, oh I'm ever so happy.

Bozenka Farr (11)
Avenue Middle School

CHOOSING PETS

Maybe a . . .
Fluffy, bouncy rabbit
   Or a . . .
Small, squeaky mouse
   Or a . . .
Snappy, sharp crocodile
   Or a . . .
Biting, barking dog
   Or a . . .
Jumpy, lumpy toad
   Or a . . .
Hissy, long snake

If I had enough pocket money
I could buy them all.

Anna Lewis (9)
Avenue Middle School

TIGERS

Striped, fast creatures,
Camouflaged in the dark green grass,
Sharp, quick,
Nice black stripes,
Cuddly, soft, furry fur,
Wild, wicked smile,
Growls in the wild,
Undercover in the undergrowth.

   Tigers

Ismail Thompson (9)
Avenue Middle School

COLOUR

Blue, do you like blue?
Blue is the swirling ocean,
Blue is the bluebell,
In spring.

Red, do you like red?
Red is the setting sun,
Red is the rosehead,
In summer.

Yellow, do you like yellow?
Yellow is the midday sun,
Yellow is the fallen leaf,
In autumn.

White, do you like white?
White is the unforgiving snow,
White is the snowdrop,
In winter.

White, yellow, red, blue,
I know what I like,
How about you?

Elliott Shaw (10)
Avenue Middle School

THE LIZARD IN A BLIZZARD

There was an old lizard,
Got caught in a blizzard.
The snow was so white,
He got blown out of sight.
And all that was left was his gizzard.

Gabriel Moore (9)
Avenue Middle School

SHADOWS ON THE MOONLIT SKY

Shadows on the moonlit sky,
Tossing, turning, don't know why;
Face to face on the moon,
Dawn will break, it will be day soon;
Almost day time, the bird will cry,
Shadows on the moonlit sky.

Shadows on the moonlit sky,
The cat has come, the bird is shy;
The caterpillar is wriggling in its cocoon,
Waiting to get a glimpse of the moon;
'Tis nigh,
Shadows on the moonlit sky.

Shadows on the moonlit sky,
The moon is like an eagle's eye;
It blossoms somewhere on a tree,
Actually it's a dancing bee;
The sun says bye,
Shadows on the moonlit sky.

Tess Little (8)
Avenue Middle School

PLAYSTATION

I'm racing round Silverstone,
Addicted, addicted.
I have a licence to kill,
Obsessed, obsessed.
Battling the Undertaker,
Can't stop, can't stop.
Can't stop playing the PlayStation.

Blythe Furness (8)
Avenue Middle School

SPACESHIP

Fire starting from under us
Jonathan making lots of fuss
The rocket starts off to the moon
But Oliver lost his spoon

We're all excited
And united
We get faster all the time
Hadden makes a new mime

Then we start slowing
And on the moon it's snowing
We get out on the moon
Around quarter past noon

We find an alien called Mossil
Then we find a great big fossil
We climb back into the ship
Jonathan gives the driver a tip

We land back down in the sea
We're back to Earth in time for tea.

Sam Bevan (9)
Avenue Middle School

CAN WE HAVE A KITTY CAT?

'Daddy, Daddy can we have a kitty cat
Huh can we please?'
'Maybe kids, I promise I'll talk about it later.'
'Daddy, Daddy can we have a kitty cat
Huh can we please?'
'No!'
'But you promised.'

Ali Tidd (9)
Avenue Middle School

I BUILT A LEGO MODEL ONCE

I built a Lego model once
The best I've ever seen,
I built a Lego model once
Blue, red and green.

I built a Lego model once,
I then went down for tea,
Extraordinary things happened,
The Lego made an agree:

'Now listen here
And let it be,
I'll build a model
And you shall see;

The tallest thing,'
Said the foes,
'We'll catapult it
And down it goes!'

Bang!
(Foes fired a cannonball)
Puff, slap, bang
Into the castle wall.

Their screams of rage
And the painful cries,
And for the foes
A little prize!

Freddie Feeney-Mellor (9)
Avenue Middle School

FOOTBALL
(Player's point of view)

Putting on my football boots,
In the dressing room,
Supporters coming to the ground,
Singing football tunes.

Chewing gum to pass the time,
'Til the match begins,
When we come out on the pitch,
The crowd begins to sing.

The teams warm up around the pitch,
Until the referee,
Blows his whistle very loud,
And starts the match at three.

At kick-off all the crowd goes crazy,
As they cheer and shout,
The ball is heading for the net,
The keeper kicks it out.

I'm standing near their goalie,
Waiting for the ball,
It's crossed to me, I head it in,
I'm feeling ten feet tall.

I pull my shirt over my head,
I punch the air with glee,
I've scored a goal, we're one-nil up,
And it's only ten past three.

We score another seven goals,
We are the greatest team,
We've won the match, we've won the cup,
It's better than any dream.

Joe Short (10)
Avenue Middle School

CHAMELEON

It hides in trees all day long,
Its eyes swivelling, looking for bugs.
In its mouth it has a flexible, extendible tongue which shoots out.
It munches, crunches, bunches of bugs,
Giving them hugs with its tongue.
Its camouflage could hide it in a ditch.
It's able to bide its time searching for the most succulent, juiciest bugs.
The trees it can lurk in, nowhere to be seen.
Suddenly, a pink flash splats on a leaf.
Its tail seems to curl into a ball.
It stays still until it perks up and slowly plods away.

Max Stankiewicz (10)
Avenue Middle School

MY BROTHER

My brother is thin, like bananas,
And he never wears pyjamas.
He likes the computer just like me,
Sometimes he can't admit he needs a wee.
My brother is a bizarre person, he hardly ever gives in,
But when he gets out of control I kick him in the shin.
I like my brother for sometimes he is nice,
But when we play a game he says, 'Let's use the dice.'
And when he says, *'Oh yes I win,'*
Mum says, 'If you don't be quiet I'll throw you in the bin!'

Gregory Seago (9)
Avenue Middle School

Books!

Books, books, glorious books!
They're excellent, wonderful and funny and great.
Harry Potter, the Moomins and Cirque Du Freak.
They're all very dangerous, you can get lost in them.

Authors must be wonderful people.
Like a dictionary they're full of ideas.
There's Rowling, Dahl and Ms Blyton too.
They've all come throughout the ages.

Romance, Adventure, Comedy and Fantasy.
They're all types of excellent books.
But when you start to read a book
You go into your own world.

Characters all have different personalities.
There's Snape - boo, hiss, no one likes him.
But then there's Dumbledore who's wise and brave
And it all levels out, for instance, the Dragon is dead.

So if you ever have any free time
Sit down and read a book
Or even much, much, much better
Snuggle up in bed with one - *sweet dreams.*

Rikk Richardson (9)
Avenue Middle School

The Sea

Waves rumble
Never seeming to crumble
They curve for a second
Before crashing to the sand.

Ships out there
All the time
Floating
Like a slice of lime.

Anna Wait (8)
Avenue Middle School

GECKOS AND GILAS

Gecko's sticky feet,
Walkin' up the wall.
Sticky, sticky feet,
Can't get off at all.

Gila's poison teeth,
Bitin' through the wood . . .
Poison, poison teeth,
. . . Could it? Yes it could.

Gecko's scaly tail,
Very long and thin.
Scaly, scaly tail,
Hidin' in the bin.

Gila's bumpy hand,
Bit like steel propellers.
Bumpy, bumpy hands,
Of those desert-dwellers.

Geckos and Gilas,
They have many features.
Some can be cruel killers,
Although they are small creatures.

Vijay Narbad (10)
Avenue Middle School

THE MIGHTY SLIDE

(Based on the poem 'The Mighty Slide' by Allan Ahlbergh)

The air was chilly,
Snow falling, all fluffy and frilly.
The children, as they danced around
The greatest slide they'd ever found.
Pitter patter of excited feet
As they waited for their go, what a treat.
Gliding like fairies in the wind,
Watching the gliders as they grinned.
Babbling, gurgling, slishing, slushing,
Come on everyone, got to keep on rushing.

Phoebe Conner (11)
Avenue Middle School

DIZZY WORLD

Grown-ups say the world spins round

But if it did then pigs would fly
Thrown across the spinning sky

And fish wake up from watery sleep
Tossed across the briny deep

The hamsters in their strawy nest
Would find it *very* hard to rest

But remember Gravity, they say
For Gravity's here to save the day.

Bennet Francis (9)
Avenue Middle School

The Storm

Waves crash against the rocks
A storm is forming
My face is wet with drops

I walk towards the sea
Down some stone steps
The storm follows me

The ground is getting slushy
I reach the sea
The sea is getting gushy

The rain is still pouring
The wind is whining
The clouds are still soaring

Suddenly sun breaks through
It is very bright
It's an amazing sight

Sofia Malik-Smith (9)
Avenue Middle School

My Cat Panda

My cat Panda is an independent cat,
You really only see him several times a day.
He watches all the birds, the mice and the frogs
In hope that he might catch some on the way.
He really is an adventurous cat
And likes to walk around the neighbourhood,
He usually fights with his brother Patch, but ends up exhausted.
All in all he is my cat!

Robert Parkin (10)
Avenue Middle School

In The Four Seasons

When I walked to school that day
The sky above was very grey,
The wind was blowing through the trees
Much, much stronger than a breeze,
Winter brings the cold and snow
Which as an ice and shiny glow,
On that cold winter night
The moon and stars were very bright.

In spring the flowers are growing
And the last cold winds are blowing,
On that first and sunny day of spring
All the birds came out to sing,
Most children went out to play
Because it was such a lovely day.

In the summer the sun is hot
And shines like a yellow burning dot,
But when it rains it gets cool again
Then the rain goes to fall in Spain,
The birds' eggs begin to hatch
And a group of boys go out to play catch,
Little chicks begin to fly
Higher and higher in the sky.

Then autumn comes and the leaves turn brown
And a little while after they start to fall down,
In this season the wind is back
And gardeners rake leaves into a stack,
Summer flowers being to die
And some lovely fruits are baked in a pie,
Once again it's the end of the year
And winter's back with Christmas cheer!

Kelsey Beezhold (8)
Avenue Middle School

A SNOWY DAY ON A SLIDE

A carpet of snow is on the ground,
It lays there in a big high mound.
The temperature's at O degrees,
And snow is covering all the trees.
The first to arrive is Alice Key,
As she goes down she screams, *'Weeee!'*

I watch her going down the slide,
It's really big, it's really wide.
Some go down screaming,
While others go down beaming.
Everyone wants to have a try,
But oh no, someone's just hurt their eye.

Everyone's really happy and gay,
But why on such a rainy day?
Who thought we could have so much fun?
When there isn't a bit of sun!

Elizabeth Rix (10)
Avenue Middle School

I AM

My legs are eight
I'm never late
I'm creepy, I crawl
I climb up the wall
I'm hairy and scary
And we all vary
I hate cold water
And I'll frighten your daughter

I am a spider!

James Harriss (8)
Avenue Middle School

MY CAT SPOT

My cat Spot is very funny
He even has a cuddly bunny,
He likes to curl up on his mat
And dreams he is a wonder cat.

His coat is as soft as silk
And under his chin as white as milk,
When you brush his back of black fur
You can be sure to make him purr.

His attitude is proud and sly
No other cat can make him cry,
He's fascinated by the fire
It's his favourite spot to retire.

He hunts robins, rats and rabbits
This is one of his horrible habits,
He has rapid razor claws
Which he disguises in velvet paws.

Even though he's sometimes barmy
He would never try to harm me,
His cute kitten looks put me under a spell
I whisper him all my secrets knowing he'll never tell.

Emily Corney (9)
Avenue Middle School

THE TRAFFIC JAM

Lorries with their big old loads
Then I saw some giant toads
All the cars were beeping wildly
Some of them were revving mildly
In the traffic jam.

People put their radios on loudly
Then I saw a smart new Audi
Pitter-patter went the rain
I'm never going there again
To the traffic jam.

Michael Webb (10)
Avenue Middle School

MY PET RABBIT, FLUFFY

I have a pet rabbit called Fluffy
And a naughty one at that
He acts all cute and causes dispute
Because he killed next door's cat

The neighbours all complained
When they found their dog dead
So I took Fluffy back
And got a shark instead

The shark was very noisy
And ate the neighbours too much
So I took my pet shark back
And got a goldfish as such

My goldfish drove the tractor
Through next door's fence
My goldfish has a high factor
Of intelli-gence

If you want to get a pet
Take my advice
Don't get a shark or a porcupine
Just get mice!

Charlie Gallacher (10)
Avenue Middle School

THE NEW MOUNTAIN BIKE

Up! Up! Up! The hill
Round the corner, past the mill
Through the forest and trees
As the bike rode by.
Past the village's little shops
And past the farmer's growing crops
To the Town Hall, now back home
As the bike rode by.
Back past the farmer's crops
Now whizzing past the shops
As the bike rode by.
Back through the forest, past the mill!
Down! Down! Down! The hill!

Sam Barker (11)
Avenue Middle School

ABOUT MY CATS

In my house there lives three cats.
The first one is Buffy,
Who is very, very fluffy.
But she hates bees.
The next one is Willow,
She's so sweet,
But she nicks my pillow.
Last of all is Smudge,
And he loves attention.
He eats anything with chocolate fudge.

Shannon Stroud (9)
Avenue Middle School

FIRE

Fire, fire it's everywhere,
Watch out, it hurts, it'll give you a scare,
People try to fight it,
But some people just ignite it,
It terrorises an entire city,
It kills people, such a pity,
Most people hate it,
But some people praise it,
They think it's dangerous and bad,
Some people like the way it flickers like mad,
People try to prevent it,
Others have tried to rent it,
It consumes within seconds,
It beckons and beckons,
The smoke is thick,
And the heat makes you sick,
It will never tire,
It's fire.

Tom Simms (11)
Avenue Middle School

A SUMMER POEM

The morning's dawned
Another day
All the children
Come out to play.
They skip and shout
As they go out.

All the children run about.

Sui Dan Wan (11)
Avenue Middle School

DINOSAURS

The dinosaur that likes to be noticed
The Don'tignorus!
The high-rise dinosaur . . .
The Multistoreysaurus!
The dinosaurs that hide in bedrooms . . .
The Chestofdrawerus!
The beach-loving dinosaur . . .
The Sandyshorus!

The dinosaur that changes its mind . . .
The Nowi'mnotsosureus!
The very uninteresting dinosaur . . .
The Goontaborus!
The dinosaur called W H Smith . . .
The Bigbookstoris!
The romantic lover . . .
The Amouramourus!
The dinosaur that cannot leave the house . . .
The Stickydoorus!
The short-sighted dinosaur . . .
The Tyrannosaurus Specs!

Thomas Kail (9)
Avenue Middle School

SNOWDROPS

Snowdrops white as crisp snow.
From far away they seem like a white woolly blanket.
They only last a week or two,
But they're still there in the soil and in my mind.

Sonia Hufton (8)
Avenue Middle School

DILL AND BILL

My bike goes down,
Down,
Down the hill.
My bike blows bubbles
With his friend
Dill.
So Dill and Bill
Go down the hill.
My bike's called Bill,
His friend is Dill.
Together they blow bubbles
Down the hill.

Sometimes my bike goes up,
Up,
Up the hill.
He blows no bubbles
For Dill is ill.
When Dill is still
Bill is sad.
When Bill is sad
He's sad and still.
Because his friend is ill.
The hill will feel sad
For no bubbles will blow.
No bubbles will
Pop!
My bike and his friend
Won't get to the
Top!

Sam Jay (9)
Avenue Middle School

WINTER WONDERS

I woke up to a whistling wind,
And had some sardines that had been tinned,
Outside I saw some blinding snow,
And I hopped on the spot, to and fro,
I walked some steps and I fell over,
In the air I could smell some Christmas clover.

A howling wind rushed through the trees
Which left behind a pile of leaves,
Lots of people were wearing hats and scarves,
And children were giving out excited laughs,
I watched Lucy and Dan have a snowball fight,
The temperature was exactly right,
Not too cold, not too hot,
And I could smell some soup, brewing in a pot.

When I got home,
My mum was on the phone,
Then she went and sat near the fire,
And then turned the heat up higher,
There was a blizzard when I went to bed,
And visions of snowmen danced in my head.

Isobel Appleton (11)
Avenue Middle School

WHEN I WENT TO THE ZOO

When I went to the zoo
I saw a monkey making fun of me,
Then I saw a polar bear sticking his tongue out at me,
Then I saw a snake hissing at me,
Then I saw an elephant squirting water at me,
All I did was laugh.

When I went to the zoo
I heard a bear growling at me,
Then I heard a lion roaring at me,
Then I heard a parrot squawking at me,
Then I heard a horse neighing at me,
Then I got a headache and went home

Samana Asif (8)
Avenue Middle School

WINTER POEM

Bright lights,
Dark nights.

Winter is almost here.

Lots of people are wearing scarves,
Lots of people are having a good laugh.

Winter is getting nearer.

Cold hands and feet,
Lots of people are wanting heat.

Winter is here!

Lots of frozen pipes,
And freezing nights.

But still a lot of Christmas cheer.

Ice is forming in the night,
People are having snowball fights.

The day before it was crisp and white,
But now it is a brown and sludgy sight.

Beth Collins (11)
Avenue Middle School

ONE FROSTY MORNING

One wintry morning,
I needed warming,
There are bright lights,
And cold windy nights
The ground was covered with snow,
And the temperatures were very low.
People wearing scarves,
Lots more laughs.
We were having a snowball fight,
When an old lady got a fright.
I found myself listening to the wind,
When I saw my friend and grinned.

Eve King (10)
Avenue Middle School

WATER

Water drips,
Water flows,
When it goes down the waterfall.
Water can be calm,
Water can be rough,
But waves can be very tough.

Water can be hot,
Water can be cold,
But can be frozen into ice,
Either way it's very nice.

Francesca Sidney (8)
Avenue Middle School

MY FRIEND REX

We're friends, me and Rex,
His hair is browny grey,
His eyes are bright blue,
He eats broccoli and vegetables and an apple on a tray,
He sits on my lap and he takes a little nap,
He's got a little pink nose and he sniffs the sweet air,
He sleeps on a bundle of straw,
My guinea pig and his friend live together in their hutch.
Rex goes, 'Chut, tweet and drr.'
My friend Rex is furry, warm and cuddly,
I love my guinea pigs, they are cosy and warm.

Sophie Kleanthous (8)
Avenue Middle School

IN MY BEDROOM LIES!

10 Smelly pairs of socks,
9   Broken shuttlecocks,
8   Pencils snapped in half,
7   Posters that make you laugh,
6   Footballs for the match today,
5   Toys chucked away,
4   Lego bits stepped on twice,
3   Board games without their dice,
2   Backpacks full of worn out conkers,
      And one, guess what?
      A person who's gone bonkers!

Holly Clarke (9)
Avenue Middle School

PLAYGROUND ACTIVITIES

Alan's arguing
Ben's bouncing
Cathy's cackling
Dan's digging
Eddy's excited
Fran's flapping
Grace's gargling
Harry's hopping
Ismail's inventing
John's jumping
Katy's kicking
Liam's laughing
Meg's moaning
Natty's niggling
Oliver's orienteering
Paul's pushing
Queeny's quarrelling
Ronald's racing
Sally's skipping
Tim's tumbling
Una's unhappy
Val's volunteering
Walter's weeping
Xena's xenophobic
Yvonne's yapping
Zak's zapping

The bell's gone
       End of play.

Alix Dixon (9)
Avenue Middle School

An Eye-Opener

My mum looks into my eyes
She knows when I tell lies
Most people read a book
But my mum can read my look
She only has to look at me
And I know she can see
Where I've been, what I've done
It really isn't any fun.

Have you seen
The teenage girls
Flutter their eyes
At the cool dude guys?
Have you seen
The clothes they wear
Big, baggy jeans
And their bellies all bare?

You should have seen
The look in my eye
When I saw Dad
In his new tie
I didn't know whether
To laugh or cry
But then I thought
Oh no, oh my
What if Dad knows
When I tell a lie?

Casey-Lee Ralph (9)
Avenue Middle School

I WOKE UP ONE MORNING

I woke up one morning
Got out of my bed
Drew back the curtains
And wandered downstairs
Then suddenly the doorbell rang
I opened the door and saw this man
The man disappeared
And in his place
Loads of things appeared
All the armies salute and say there'll be no wars
Some animals came up to me and spoke without words
The sun was shining
And the air smelt delicious
For there was no more pollution
No one ever died
No burglars
No murderers
No criminals whatsoever
Everything was perfect
Nothing went wrong
I woke up one morning
Got out of my bed
And discovered it was all a dream

Catherine Bundy (9)
Avenue Middle School

MY DOG MILLY

My dog Milly, chews a lot of things,
Whatever you have she wants to chew,
But she is still my favourite pet,
I would not change her, not yet!

Beth Ash (8)
Avenue Middle School

IF I COULD CHOOSE A PET . . .

If I could choose a pet,
I would pick a dog,
Or maybe a frog,
But then I might be slimy.

If I could choose a pet,
I would love a cat,
Or maybe a rat,
But then again it might have thick, creepy tail.

If I could choose a pet,
I would adore a hare,
Or maybe a bear,
Then again it might eat me.

If I could choose a pet,
I would go for a foal,
Or maybe a mole,
But then again it might go under next door's fence.

But in the end, I would probably choose a guinea pig called Violet,
Because she chose me!

Georgia Barker (10)
Avenue Middle School

SALSABIL

Salsabil's colour is yellow, as bright as the sun.
She is as pretty as the most beautiful flowers.
Salsabil is a jolly bouncy sort of person who can always cheer you up.
Salsabil's fruit is an apple because it is sweet and rosy red.
She is sunny hot weather.
I see her sitting with her friends giggling and laughing.
Even though she can be silly she'll always be my friend.

Madinah Thompson (9)
Avenue Middle School

STARS

Stars glisten in the sky,
Watch the shooting ones fly,
See them sparkle,
See them twinkle,
Stars, stars, stars.

Stars shine big and bright,
Shining in the black of night,
See them glow,
See them glint,
Stars, stars, stars.

Stars are wonderful, see them shine,
They're so wonderful I wish they were mine,
See them shining,
See some gliding,
Stars, stars, stars.

Amy Fitch (10)
Avenue Middle School

SHOWER

Who fires these arrows into my pond?
Who sends these spears from somewhere beyond?
Sharp as a razor, faster than light,
Splinters of crystal come out of the night.

Who are they after, what do they want?
Who are they hunting, how can we blunt
These silvery needles, darting and slick?
Will one of them find me? Shelter me quick!

Dungeons of bubbles, wriggling through chains
Down to deep water, dark murky panes.
Suddenly everything's peaceful and mute.
Up to the surface rises the newt.

Hal Rutherford (9)
Avenue Middle School

SPACE

Don't be scared
It's only true,
Just keep it a secret
Between me and you.

We think we're safe
Here on our little Earth,
But we may collide
With a comet giving birth.

We don't have a clue
So many asteroids out there,
Going their own way
That some people can't bear.

How would you feel?
Safe in your bed,
Suddenly told we all
Could be dead!

But wait, maybe all is not lost
Scientists launch a huge rocket,
It speeds towards the comet
And hitting it off course, they knock it.

Catherine Bridgman (8)
Avenue Middle School

Auntie Anna's Angry Alligator...

Auntie Anna's angry Alligator
Bought a big baby Ball
Caught a coughing Cat
Danced a Devon Dance
Enjoyed an Elephant eating
Fought a fiendish Fight
Gave a generous Gift
Heard a happy Hog
Itched an itchy Itch
Jinxed a juicy Jeweller
Kicked a keen Koala
Licked a lovely Lolly
Managed to make a Meringue
Nursed a nice Newt
Observed an orange Orang-utan
Peeled a purple Pear
Questioned a quivering Quail
Recognised a Rabbit relative
Saw a selfish Swordfish
Treated a Tiger to tea
Uncovered an ugly Ulcer
Vexed a Victorian Vicar
Watched a wicked Witch
X-rayed an Xmas Xylophone
Yapped a yippee Yow!
And
Zapped a zigzag Zebra.

Isobel Emberson (10)
Avenue Middle School

MY CAT RALPH

My best friend is Ralph, my cat,
Go too near him and you'll get a bat!
But if *pat* is all you give,
He will surely let you live.

Ralph's been given many names:
Prushka, Malcolm, Frank and James.
You won't want to hear the rest,
Ralph just seemed to suit him best.

Ralph my cat is snowy white,
With little grey patches, dark and light.
There's a sad look in his eyes,
He could surely win a prize.

When a flash of light is seen,
Both his eyes shine bright and green:
He jumps around and tries to pounce,
Though it doesn't weigh an ounce.

Ralph plays with his catnip mouse,
Chasing it around the house.
He does lots of funny things:
Hides in cupboards, goes in bins.

He likes any kind of food,
When he's feeling in the mood.
Chicken, pilchards, milk and cheese,
Sweetcorn, mushrooms, chips and peas.

My best friend is Ralph, my cat,
Go too near him and you'll get a bat!
But if *pat* is all you give,
He will surely let you live.

Matthew Drake (10)
Avenue Middle School

THE SEA CAT

The curly swirly wave
That hits the rocky beach
The sea cat, the sea cat

The frightening storm
The smooth sea
The sea cat, the sea cat

As rough as gravel
As still as glass
The sea cat, the sea cat

Sometimes pouncing
At small ships
The sea cat, the sea cat

People come to watch the cat
That just repeats and repeats its moves
The sea cat, the sea cat

Kate Lacey (9)
Avenue Middle School

FLOWERS

Flower in the garden
Flower in a pot.
Flower by the river
What a pretty spot!
Petunias and gardenia
Don't forget forget-me-nots
Daisies in the garden
Tie them in knots!

Grace Leeder (8)
Avenue Middle School

TRAFFIC JAMS!

Someone picking their nose
A girl trying to doze
A woman watering her lawn
A baby newborn
A man shouting
Two ladies pouting
One plastic model of Po
Three cardboard aliens in a window
A small village fair
A baby clutching its teddy bear
Eight people walking the dogs
A Dutch lady wearing clogs
Someone playing on a Game Boy
An Irishman shouting, 'Oy, oy.'
    In the traffic jam!

Rosie Fullwood-Thomas (9)
Avenue Middle School

THE STRONG THORN

When I was cycling
A strong thorn gave me a puncture.

So upside down goes the bike
Out come the tools
And off comes the wheel.

Then I saw a very small thorn
That had gone straight through such a thick tyre
And inner tube
And was not blunt but still sharp
Like a nail.

Billy McKibben (9)
Avenue Middle School

THE BIG MATCH

On the day when the people were waiting
And in the shops the bookies were rating
In the changing rooms the coaches shout
Whilst outside the fans mingle in and out
'Hooray! Hooray! The big match is today.'
The teams run out, one blue, one red
The captains shook hands, David and Ted
Then the ref came through the doors
And he blew the whistle and there were giant roars
'Hooray! Hooray! The big match is today.'

They passed the ball around the pitch
And eventually a goal was snitched
All of that team ran around the ground
And all the supporters made a tremendous sound
'Hooray! Hooray! The big match is today.'
But then the opponents got one back
The goal was made by a brilliant attack
And their celebrations were basically the same
But then the match stopped because half-time came
'Hooray! Hooray! The big match is today.'

In the first five minutes another goal was scored
And the opposition's crowd were getting really loud
The opponents had the ball again
Would another goal save the game?
'Hooray! Hooray! The big match is today.'
Would another goal be seen today?
Or would the game be called a bad play?
With five minutes to go the score was 2-1
And time whooshed past and the full time whistle had gone
'Hooray! Hooray! The big match has been played.'

After the match had been played
And all the money had been made
The people were going to their cars
Or coming out the bars
'Hooray! Hooray! The big match has been played.'
When the people were back from Rome
And all warm and cosy in their home
On the news on the TV
Someone was shouting, 'That's me, that's me!'

Josh Swan (9)
Avenue Middle School

THE TRAFFIC LIGHT POEM

Three wonderful colours of the rainbow
Has the traffic light,
Green means go,
To keep the flow,
Of traffic that's in flight.
When amber shows,
It tells the flow,
You really must slow down.
Red's on top,
You must stop!
Or else a siren will come
With a cop.

In my opinion,
Lights are the law
Of the highway,
That was never there before.

Andrew Longhurst (10)
Avenue Middle School

THE COOLEST KID

Elvis is the coolest kid, what if he left! Heaven forbid!
He strides along the corridors,
Girls grovel and kneel on the those sacred floors.
Elvis is the coolest kid, what if he left! Heaven forbid!
But the only girl he's interested in is Martha-May,
In her delightful way,
Doing the catwalk,
Not stopping to talk, only to Elvis, the coolest kid!

Elvis is the coolest kid, what if he left! Heaven forbid!

Mary Collins (9)
Avenue Middle School

MY DOUGHNUT

I lift it from my plate
All big and round
And then I hear the sound
Of sugar grinding on my teeth
Then out pops the jam
Dribbling all over my chin.

I do a big grin
And ask Mum,
'Is there anything on my mouth?'

'Not really,' said Mum,
'Just the best part of a doughnut, that's all!'

Lauren Cutter (9)
Avenue Middle School

WAITING

Waiting, waiting
Waiting for the bus
Hurry up, hurry up
I'm in a rush

Waiting, waiting
Waiting for my friend
We've got to do a project
And we're nowhere near the end

Waiting, waiting
Waiting for the end of school
I'm so excited
'Cause I'm going to the pool

Waiting, waiting
Waiting for the train
Hurry up, hurry up
It's starting to rain

Waiting, waiting
Waiting for the loo
My sister's on the toilet
And I'm desperate for a poo

Waiting, waiting
Waiting for my dad
Hurry up, hurry up
This waiting's driving me *mad!*

Sophie Holland (10)
Avenue Middle School

A SUCCESSFUL TRIP ACROSS THE ROAD

It all started when I got home from school
Me and my friend playing pool
And I hit the ball as hard as I can
Meanwhile my friend goes *bamm*
I go, 'Oh yes, I win the game,'
My friend says, 'Well done,' in shame.
The disco's today, Oh! Yes Oh! Yes.

My mum calls me and my friend for tea
And I run down the stairs with lots of glee
My friend calling, 'Wait up! Wait up!'
But I'm sorry I can't stop!
The disco's today Oh! Yes Oh! Yes!

My friend leaves in a flurry to be back by a time
I start to say something but it turns into a mime
So I go upstairs to get ready
Run to my room and stop steady
My mum calls, 'Ned, are you ready?'
The disco's today Oh! Yes Oh! Yes.

My brother comes up to me and says, 'Hey Ned,
Maybe you could dye your hair red.'
So I dyed my hair
With lots of flair
So I went downstairs to the cloakroom
To find my mum sweeping up with a broom
The disco's today Oh! Yes Oh! Yes.

And I ring up my friend
And drive him round the bend
I say, 'I'll meet you at yours at twenty-past five,
Stay cool and keep alive.'
The disco's today Oh! Yes Oh! Yes.

I go and my mum said, 'Be careful on the road.'
So down the road I strode
To the great, big Earlham Road
A boy saying, 'Hey Ned! Hey Ned!'
But I didn't hear the boy
The disco's today Oh! Yes Oh! Yes.

So I get to the lights
When it's just turned night?
I press the button hard
Walk halfway across the road
And
Bang! Crash! Wallop!
Where am I? Where am I?
'Ned, Ned, It's all right, you're OK.'

Who are all the people?
Where am I? Where am I?
You are going to hospital
Yes the disco's today - *thud!*

Ned Lamb (9)
Avenue Middle School

MY LIFE

When I was . . .

> One I was the first.
> Two I only burst.
> Three I learned how to pee.
> Four I ate the dog's door.
> Five I was allowed to drive.
> Six I ran the grand prix.
> Seven I moved to Devon.
> Eight I was used as bait.

Jonathan Trick (8)
Avenue Middle School

WOULD YOU CALL A SPIDER HAIRY LEGS IF YOU CROSSED HIS WEB?

Would you call a spider,
Hairy legs?

Would you call a spider,
Creepy legs?

Would you call a spider,
Long legs?

Would you call a spider,
Tickly legs?

Would you call a spider,
Scary legs?

But wait till you cross,
His web.

If you do, his

Hairy
Creepy
Long
Tickly
Scary legs

Will wrap around you
And suck your blood!

Sophie Perks (9)
Avenue Middle School

In The Middle Of The Deep Blue Sea

In the middle of the deep blue sea
Seals play peacefully,
Dolphins dive with ease and grace,
Whales pass with cheerful face,
Shoals of fish swim all around
Into a treasure chest not yet found,
An octopus wriggles, his eight legs winding,
A crab goes on his seashell finding,
A jellyfish floats up to the surface.
What's left? There's one we've missed.
Ah! The lovely starfish!
The starfish lies luxuriously
On a rock deep under the sea.

Ellen Sharpe (9)
Avenue Middle School

Space

Whooshing, swirling, twisting space.
Twinkling stars dance with grace,
Whooshing, swirling, twisting space.
Rockets thread through planets like lace,
Whooshing, swirling, twisting space.
Stars fly as if in a whirling chase,
Whooshing, swirling, twisting space.
Magical mystic place,
Whooshing, swirling, twisting space!

Marie Sabec (10)
Avenue Middle School

TRAFFIC JAMS

Someone swearing in a car, across the road a German spa
An English choir saying 'La' in the traffic jam.

A baby crying in his cot, an old man's teeth about to rot
On the road a big dark spot, in the traffic jam.

A man hooting, getting hot, a woman's kitchen, boiling hot
Someone else saying, 'Not,' in the traffic jam.

An old woman on the road and then I saw a giant toad
We're going down Baker's Road in the traffic jam.

Ben driving a Yamaha about to wreck your car
You say 'Hi ya' in the traffic jam.

Fumes rising from a car, no one likes my jam jar
They think it is a bright star.

Red lights all around, yellow lights, very round,
Green lights west bound, in the traffic jam.

I thought I heard a gong, the traffic jam was gone.

Kieran Beezhold (10)
Avenue Middle School

TOMMY

My rabbit Tommy I love him so much,
When I stroke him he's lovely to touch,
I'd cuddle him close with such a clutch,
He's the best pet.

His fur is soft and very neat,
His little eyes are so sweet,
Carrots and lettuce for him to eat,
He's the best pet.

But now he's gone and run away,
And I don't know what to say,
His hutch is empty where he lay,
He was the best pet.

Beth Loaker (9)
Avenue Middle School

THE COOL SKATEBOARD

It was my birthday and I was ten
My mum and dad let me choose my gift
I knew what I wanted right there and then
A cool dude skateboard from the ship called Drift.

First I had to choose a real good deck
I found one with a picture on made by Blind
It took all my money but what the heck
And my mum and dad said they didn't mind.

A skateboard without wheels
Is just a plank of wood
A skateboard without wheels
Is not a lot of good.

So next I chose some wheels which are very, very fast
Some grip for the top to stop me slipping off
I will be just a blur as I go whizzing past
Doing tailslides, kickflips and lots of other stuff.

I will learn how to ollie
I will learn how to grind
I will be extremely jolly
Doing stunts of every kind.

If you enjoyed my poem you may applaud
This was the story of the cool skateboard.

Jacob Conner (10)
Avenue Middle School

HISTORY

History starts right here a long, long time ago.
With deadly dinosaurs *stomping!* Steadily.
Next there's grubby cavemen crouching and killing their food to
        stay alive.
The Egyptians with mummies buried with their treasure.
Then there's groovy Greeks battling all the Persians.
The vicious Vikings were plump and ploppy like pigs.
Next there's Henry VIII who had no faith in marriage
But was so fat he couldn't ride in a carriage.
After that there's cowboys and Indians who killed billions of people.
And that's the end of a not so boring *history!*

Phillip Sadd (10)
Avenue Middle School

CLOWNS

Clowns are clumsy, cheeky, clever
Very, very lazy, laughter, little, large
And loud as can be.

Weird, wacky, wonderful
The funniest wigs you ever did see.

They talk nonsense, very noisy
And *big, red noses,* silly, sad
Shocking, sneaky, smelly
Sometimes short, sometimes tall
That's what clowns can be.

Leanne Lee (10)
Avenue Middle School

THE MOUSE

Little mouse
In the house
Searching for a
Tasty louse
When she finds one
Eats it up
Then she searches
For a cup
Makes herself a
Cup of tea
Drinks it down with
So much glee
Then she puts
Herself to bed
Time to rest her
Sleepy head.

Polly Gilham (10)
Avenue Middle School

EARTH WITHOUT SUN

Wake up one morning
Look out of your window
You are horror-struck
There is no plant life
Just torn earth
You feel sick with pain
Suddenly you feel sad and empty

The Earth is a hopeless wreck.

William Tiddy (10)
Avenue Middle School

MY FAVOURITE THINGS

Curling up by the fire on Friday nights
To watch Buffy and friends and have a fright
Holidays in hot countries without spiders that bite

The feeling when the school term ends
And meeting lots of new friends
Going out for pizzas at the weekends

Chocolate and ice cream, sausages and chips
Dancing on the stage and swinging my hips
Tasting strawberry lip gloss on my lips

Watching 'Little Vampire' with my brother
Counting the dolphins on my duvet cover
Cuddling up with my teddies and especially my mother

Twizzling around on the swizzle chair
Doing nice things with my long brown hair
Going to Cambridge for the Strawberry Fair

My best friend Rosie who I've known since I was two
Jacqueline Wilson's books too
I think that will have to do!

Rhianna Ellington (9)
Avenue Middle School

SIR PERCIVAL

Sir Percival was a knight who gave me a bit of a fright,
His sword was as broad as my dad's Ford.
Sir Percival was so gallant and bold,
And won many battles so I've been told.

His horse was called Frank, he was long, lean and lank,
And between you and me, he stank.
There he rode throughout the land,
How great Sir Percival was in those stories of old.

William Snowden-Crate (9)
Avenue Middle School

MY RAT

If you have a nose, a wet black nose,
    I know what you must be.
A big black, dirty, smelly rat,
    As coal black as can be.

Your whiskers and tail are twitching,
    Your fur is soft and fair.
You are a most elegant rat,
    A rat beyond compare.

I know your nose is very long,
    And I know you're very nosy.
You creep inside of people's houses,
    By the fire all snug and cosy.

You aren't a very caring rat,
    You have a heart of cement.
But I happen to love you dearly Fang,
    And think you're excellent.

To us a sewer's a horrible place,
    But to you it is a home.
I'd love to be a rat sometimes,
    Because you are never alone!

Beth Hipwell (11)
Avenue Middle School

SEASONS IN THE GARDEN

Spring is exciting
Spring is new
Spring is when
The buds burst through

Then comes summer
Warm and bright
The garden looks
A wondrous sight

Autumn is when
The trees turn bare
The wind blows leaves
High in the air

Winter is cold
And nothing grows
The ground is covered
With a layer of snow

Camilla Pendleton (10)
Avenue Middle School

I AM LIKE

I am like a blade of grass covering the land
I am like a small seashell lying on the sand
I am like a lily pad resting on the sea
I am like a tiny bird sleeping in a tree
I am like a small white cloud floating in the sky
I am like a summer's breeze gently passing by
I am like the silver moon sailing across the night
I am like the golden sun shining with delight.

Tania Sluckin (9)
Avenue Middle School

SHIP SONG

Me and my ship, ship, ship
Go out to have some fish and chips
Just my boat and me
Going out to sea
The big, big waves go out to the shore
But my boat and me want more, more, more!
People wonder if we'll ever come back
But we are still on track!

Isabel Davies (8)
Avenue Middle School

FIRST DAY AT SCHOOL

I've arrived at school
Everybody's here
My mum's gone and left me
I'm full of fear
Here comes my teacher

I hope she's very kind
I hope she helps me with my work
I hope she doesn't mind
I am only little
There's big people here

I only hope they like me
I only hope they care
In the end it all worked out
And my teacher didn't have to shout.

Rebecca Buck (10)
Bawburgh CP School

THE HIJACKER

Looking up I see
A large metal container!
A sardine tin
Bright yellow and orange!

Shivers run through me
I'm really scared.
Thoughts of my cousin and sun
Help my phobic thoughts of sinking.

Fists of hail smash against me
And the bright yellow hull
Up the gang plank I go
Really, really scared.

The hail is not ceasing
Nor are my fears.
We're up on board
The sardine tin.

My stomach is rumbling
With fear and hunger.
I go into the carpeted container
And buy some worm droppings in worms!

I'm really, really scared now,
Ow! That hurt!
Help! Help! The container's being hijacked
And we are prisoners.

Oh phew! It's boiling in this container of a ship!
Help!
Oh! You're a constable
Help me please, oh *please!*

Phew! Thank you! Thank you!
Thank you sergeant!

Madeline Green-Armytage (10)
Bawburgh CP School

I HAVE A MAGIC SPELL BOOK

I have a magic spell book.
It really scares me.
I do not want to look.
I just don't want to see.
I know it sounds stupid.
But it's very, very true.
It looks very hard.
And I do not have a clue.

I am frightened what I will do.
I'm scared of what I will see.
Nevertheless I am going to open it
With the golden key.

I have opened the magic spell book
With the golden key.
Spells rushing all over the place.
It terrified me.
I am glad I opened the spell book.
I am really quite proud.
There was nothing to be scared of.
Not even a crowd.

Emma Ragan (10)
Bawburgh CP School

THE JOURNEY

The weather is wet
The weather is rough
The weather is splashing
The weather is strong
The rain is swaying
The weather is blinding
The ship is rocking
The sea is blue
The hail is hitting the side of the ship
The size of bricks
Crashing and banging
Like thunder and lightning
What shall I do?
Finish the journey or jump overboard?

William Lee (11)
Bawburgh CP School

JOURNEY TO JUPITER

Planets, stars and galaxies are whooshing past me.
My all enclosing glass bubble gives me a vision of space.

Jupiter awaits to show its *red, orange and white* circular rings to me.
A *massive* colourful planet full of gas to fill my satisfaction
and to kill off my nerves.

As I push down harder on my scooter
It makes me tumble even more
Missing people like me as I'm enjoying the satisfaction of my ride.

Ben Radford (11)
Bawburgh CP School

THE NIGHTMARE COME TRUE

I see it rocking, a huge wooden length of a ship
It makes me lose my sense
I'm terrified, I'm petrified, I don't want to go!

I'm cold, I'm wet and we're now about to go
I'm scared, worried, worried and I'm excited but nervous too
And my feet feel like ice

My nose is making a puddle on the ship
It's rocking and I'm wet and cold

At last I'm back home now
Oh no, move over
I'm now going to make a different kind of puddle.

Holly Topsom (10)
Bawburgh CP School

THE THING IN OUR BACK GARDEN

Hear the noises that the spaceship's making
The roaring, banging as the spaceship's landing
Look at the door, here come the crew
They're big
Slimy
They come as blue
It can't be real! Stop messing around
We know it's really you!

Nathan Shreeve Smith (10) & Nicholas Francis (9)
Bawburgh CP School

THE SPIDERS IN MY ROOM

I really hate spiders
The worst bit is their legs
When they crawl upon your arm
They start to spin a web

I found myself quite calm
When the spider crawled up my arm
It was rather large
So I tried to shout for my mother Marge
After that I've never been frightened
Of the spiders in my room.

Victoria Ragan (10)
Bawburgh CP School

UP AND AWAY

I'm in my seat, I'm ready to go.
We're on the ground so very low.
We'll soon be high, touching the sky.
    But hey, we're just about to fly.

We're in the sky so very high.
Seeing the angels as they fly by.
I'll never fly so very high.
Till the day I die, die, die.

I'm just about to land.
Hey look, there's some sand.
I'm starting to see the sea.
    Hey, there's a key.

Nadia O'Brien (11)
Bawburgh CP School

WASHING MACHINE

Splish, splash, splosh goes my washing machine.
Splish, splash, splosh my mummy's going out.
Splish, splash, splosh, splish, splash, splosh.
What should I do?
What should I do?
Hurry up Mum, hurry up Mum
Before it goes splat!
It's gone everywhere.

Stacey Gibb (10)
Bawburgh CP School

MY MAGIC BOX

I will put in the box . . .
A fiery red feather from a burning phoenix.
A short hair from a mystical unicorn.
The long neck of a prehistoric Diplodocus.

I will put in the box . . .
A razor-sharp claw of the darkest green dragon.
A cold swing of a Pterondon's enormous wing.
The coldness of the darkest night of the darkest planet.

I will put in the box . . .
Ripples on the clearest water from a flying fish.
Some horrible green slime of the scariest monster.
The last and loudest bark of a lovely golden retriever.

I will put in the box . . .
A sharp scale of a three-eyed fish.
The inside of an ear listening to the deafening cry of a hideous banshee.
The buzz of a tiny little bee flying.

Trystan Watts (10)
Great Witchingham VA Primary School

MY MAGIC BOX

I will put in my box . . .
One thousand stars from the never-ending universe.
The flashing reflections of running water.
The blinding light at the end of the tunnel.

I will put in my box . . .
The cunning of the speedy wolf, racing through the forest.
The echoing growl of the towering dragon.
The creepy shadows in the corners of dark libraries.

I will put in my box . . .
The chime from an ancient clock striking twelve.
The cheer of the crowd as the ball hits the back of the net.
The shining blade of the swift samurai.

Miles Robertson (10)
Great Witchingham VA Primary School

MY MAGIC BOX

I will put in the box . . .
The first speck of light for a newborn baby.
The swipe of a ball flying into the back of a football net.
The splash of people diving into the water.

I will put in the box . . .
The last baa of an ancient sheep.
A first blow of a spacecraft.
The first leap of the first astronaut leaping on the moon.

I will put in the box . . .
The first swipe of meat in a dinosaur's mouth.
The laugh of a very best friend.
The first bang of a scientist blowing up his chemistry lab.

William Powles (9)
Great Witchingham VA Primary School

MY MAGIC BOX

I will put in the box . . .
The slippery surface of a dog's nose.
Light beaming out of a crack in the door.
The desperate roar of an abandoned lion cub.

I will put in the box . . .
The 'meep' of a newly born guinea pig.
The darkness of a deep, black hole.
The glowing fire, golden and red.

I will put in the box . . .
An ear splitting scream from a haunted mansion.
The sun beaming down on a natural blue lake.
The gleaming glow of a polished mirror.

My box is fashioned from bronze, gold and silver,
With peacocks on the lid and smiles in the corners.
The hinges are made of unicorn's hair.

I will fly in my box forever and land on a feather cushion.

Vita Sunter (9)
Great Witchingham VA Primary School

MY MAGIC BOX

I will put in my box . . .
A clock going tick tock.
A cat waggling its tail.
A flick of a book going to the end of its journey.

I will put in the box . . .
Lights going on and off in a storm.
Some birds flying south for the winter.
A star shining out in the sky.

Lucy Bower (10)
Great Witchingham VA Primary School

MY MAGIC BOX

I will put in the box . . .
A waddle of a penguin on a frosty day.
The soft and silky swish of a peacock feather.
The mystical ring of Saturn.

I will put in the box . . .
The spot of a cheetah as it runs as fast as lightning.
The long beak of a hummingbird.
The rock hard shell of a tortoise.

I will put in the box . . .
A blade of grass from the finest meadow.
The twinkle of a star on a pitch-black night.
The first snowflake of a cold winter.

My box is made of glass, ice and water.
It's got every planet on the lid,
Its hinges are made from birds wings.

I shall sleep and live in my box forever and ever.

Sarah Burton (10)
Great Witchingham VA Primary School

MY MAGIC BOX

I will put in the box . . .
The moonlight shining bright.
The first brown teddy I ever had.
The rain falling onto the house roof, pitter, patter.

I will put in the box . . .
Snow falling round the house.
My first whippet called Max.
The Christmas bells ringing.

Katie Symonds (10)
Great Witchingham VA Primary School

MY MAGIC BOX

I will put in the box . . .
The last purr of my cat.
The first bloom of spring.
A memory of a dog barking.

I will put in the box . . .
The first sprinkle of snow.
The last leaves off a tree.
The first bleat of a newborn lamb.

Faye Walker (10)
Great Witchingham VA Primary School

EXCITEMENT

Excitement is the colour of bright, blue sky,
It smells like your birthday cake,
It tastes like warm caramel,
It sounds like a giggle from your baby sister,
It makes you feel anxious inside.
Excitement lives in a blindfold.

Joshua Walker (9)
Gresham Village School

THERE WAS A YOUNG MAN CALLED CHESTER

There was a young man called Chester,
Who adored the town of Leicester,
He said with a grin,
'It's the town I live in'
That stupid young lad called Chester.

Jessica Kerr (9)
Gresham Village School

SILENCE IN THE CLASSROOM

Silence in the classroom,
No noise except the chair creaking,
Like a rusty bike,
It creaks steadily like a mouse squeaking.

Somebody is stirring,
The teacher will hunt you down,
A person whispering,
A pencil plopping on the floor,
No noise now.

Silence in the dinner hall,
No noise except somebody devouring their lunch box,
Munching of crisps, crack
Slurping of a drink.

Cobwebs glinting in the blazing sun,
A clatter of children leave the hall,
All is still,
Dust sweeps across the hall
No noise now.

Natasha Lloyd (11)
Gresham Village School

TOUCH

Touch!
What can you feel?
The prickly spines of a hibernating hedgehog
The cold stem of a winter leaf,
The rough body of a log.

Touch!
What can you feel?
The slimy body of a worm,
The thousands of legs of a centipede that squirms!

Thomas Britton (8)
Gresham Village School

IF I WENT ON HOLIDAY

If I went on holiday I would travel to the bottom of the Atlantic Ocean,
I'd swim through the slimy, slippery seaweed,
Roam past restive, romantic rainbowfish and
Snorkel in and out of the sunken, shivering shipwrecks.
Or
If I went on holiday I would travel to the Egyptian desert,
I'd prowl over every proud, perfect pyramid,
Crawl through crackly, crunching caves and
Scurry over soft, silvery sand.
Or
If I went on holiday I would travel to the South American rainforest,
I'd tackle the tall, tough trees,
Slither along with the sneaky, scaly snakes and
Move when I see a mindless, mischievous monkey.
Or
If I went on holiday I would travel to the Swiss Alpine mountains
I'd view the vast, verdant valleys,
Call in at every constructed, colourful café and
Meander up the massive, musical mountains.
Or
I'll just stay here!

Debbie Holt (10)
Gresham Village School

THE HAUNTED HOUSE

I walk up the cold, stone steps
I open the door
It creaks
Am I alone or not?
I look around
Nothing to be seen
The door shuts
Was it the wind
Or was it something else.
Am I alone or not?
I feel a cold draught pass my face
Am I alone or not?
Crash!
I'm terrified
Of what I might find
In the other room.
Am I alone or not?
What a relief
It's only a jackdaw
Why was I afraid?
I am alone.
Then I hear a noise
Bump, bump, bump!
It's coming up the stairs
Am I alone or not?
It's in the doorway
Bump!
Help! I'm not alone.

Kerry Kinsley (9)
Gresham Village School

I WISH . . .

I wish that I was Tarzan
I'd swing from tree to tree,
Maybe I'd play with monkeys,
And fly up with the bees.

No - I wish I was a mermaid,
I'd swim down to the depths,
Maybe I'd find an octopus,
Come up gasping for breath.

No - I wish I was a pirate,
I'd sail a pirate ship,
I'd have to have a treasure map,
And get the treasure quick.

No - I wish that I was Shakespeare,
I'd make plays day and night,
Othello, Hamlet and Macbeth,
I'd write and write and write.

No - I wish I was a popstar,
A Spice Girl I would be
Sporty, Scary, Posh, Mel B,
Which is the one for me?

But it is rather hard to be,
In someone else's shoes,
To think and write and talk like them,
I wonder which you'd choose!

Deborah Wrighton (10)
Gresham Village School

MISTY

Misty, Misty go away,
You fight me and claw me,
Until the thunderstorm breaks!

Hooray, hooray, you've gone,
And the sun has come out,
Good Little Misty . . .
'Whoopsey!'

Oh no I called him Little Misty,
So now he's out again,
Because he doesn't like me
Calling him Little Misty.

Sorry, I haven't explained
Myself very well have I,
Because I'm Luke and I can never
Go outside because Misty is there.

Finally I'm in my swimming pool,
Because it is lovely and burning hot;
It has probably melted Misty, and
Suddenly from out of nowhere . . .

Roar!
I dashed to get my clothes,
It was him, it was Misty again.

The strange thing was that
When I came back out the sun was shining brighter than ever
I shouted
Yes the sun and Misty have had a fight,
And the sun has won!

Samantha Bayle (10)
Gresham Village School

THE WINTER WONDERLAND

In the winter snow
Frosty ice
Is amazingly nice
And hearts are bursting with hopefulness
But as the day draws through
The whiteness fades
And it's back to taxes and bills that haven't been paid.

Sophie Cowper Johnson (10)
Gresham Village School

BREAKFAST

Mum is cooking breakfast
We start the moaning.
'Muumm he's nicked my bread.'
'He ate my bacon.'
'Can I have a drink?'
'He kicked me.'
'No I didn't.'
'Yes you did.'
Mum says 'Shut up and eat up'
So we shut up and eat up
Then we start moaning again
'I'm full up.'
'Can I put the TV on?'
'Can I listen to some music?'
'I want more bacon.'
'I'm still hungry.'
Mum's going to shout
'Right if you two don't stop your moaning you won't have anything
                                                    at all.'
'OK, OK.'
'Can I have a drink please?'

Christopher Barlow (10)
Neatishead VC Primary School

MY BED

Each night in my warm bed
Different dreams run through my head
And as I sleep,
You can't hear a peep.

Dreams of Christmas,
Dreams of snow,
When dreams are gone,
Where do they go?

Each night, I tuck up tight,
With sometimes a terrible fright
But sometimes I dream of yummy ice cream
Which guides me through the night.

Lauren Simpson (9)
Neatishead VC Primary School

SCHOOLS

Primary school is a prison for kids under twelve,
The uniforms are fitted for little green elves,
The spaghetti tastes of cheesy worms,
We just can't wait until our spring term,
Our teachers are aliens from outer space
They have twenty-four eyes and an ugly face
Assemblies are boring it makes me weep
If it goes on any longer I'll fall asleep
Home time is when they ring the bell
Grab your bags and run like hell!

Dominic McIntyre (11)
Neatishead VC Primary School

BUGS

Some bugs eat leaves,
Some bugs eat trees.
Others just hang around,
And wait for bees.

Some like to look pretty,
Like moths and butterflies.
Some are extra greedy,
And steal people's pies!

Others just like to be happy,
And sit and smile and sing.
But I have always liked the lot,
As much as anything.

Lewis Clinch (8)
Neatishead VC Primary School

CHOCOLATE

Chocolate is so sweet
It is a lovely treat
It makes my mouth water
And it only cost a quarter.
Oh chocolate is so lovely
And it's sometimes bubbly
It smells nice but not like spice
It's very nice
When it melts it gives you a taste
That I wouldn't waste
I love chocolate.

Stephanie Culling (9)
Neatishead VC Primary School

THE COUNTRYSIDE

The long wide countryside,
Lay still,
As I pass a windmill.
I stand, I stare,
Why is there no one there?
The farmer's out ploughing the land,
Until it's cut smooth and bland.
The red sky prepares for night,
No sign of day, no sign of light.

Night has come, the sky is black,
Where squirrels hide their nuts I sat.
As an owl flies by,
I see a rat, how peaceful he lies.
A slight breeze tickles my skin,
A mosquito buzzes by, how pathetically thin.
Dust to dawn,
The farmer sees his yellow corn.
The sun shines this hot day,
Let's see what nature brings this May.

Nicola Shattock (11)
Notre Dame Preparatory School

THE CHOCOLATE SHOP

Every shop I go in
There's chocolate everywhere
Chocolate cakes, chocolate bars
And a tasty chocolate bear.

I went into the shop,
To buy a chocolate cake,
There I saw a man
Who said it had just been baked.

Every shop I go in,
There's chocolate everywhere,
All the fun I have,
In a chocolate chair!

Emily Ticehurst (9)
Notre Dame Preparatory School

THE SMUGGLER'S TREASURE

As pirates and smugglers
Conquer the shore
A hungry seagull
Makes an eerie caw.

They're looking for treasure
The X marks the spot
Staring at the map
Studying every dot.

Take twenty paces north
And five paces west
You should have found some treasure
Now to find the rest.

You will find the treasure
In a dirty, mouldy chest
When you get all the riches
You'll think that you're the best.

When you get home
You must guard the riches
You must hide from the law
That's just one of the hitches.

Nathan Goose (11)
Notre Dame Preparatory School

THE TEARING HORSE

I saw a tearing horse running through the field
It was so lovely I wanted to go and see it
It was soft, furry and cute
It had a black and white coat
I had a little dream of riding on that horse
Winning a golden trophy
The time I went on that horse my life changed
From riding on that beautiful horse
I love my life
I will grow up to train a horse
And ride one too
So here is my story
Just waiting for you.

Francesca Stafford-Pelham (8)
Notre Dame Preparatory School

MY PET DOG

My pet dog is very sweet
She likes to bark, play and eat
She guards at night and keeps me safe
And in the morning she's wide awake
She plays with her ball and runs about
Then I hear Mum give a shout
We take her to the park
She runs like a flame
She has a great time
She ran round the bend and met a new friend.

Nicole Oakley (8)
Notre Dame Preparatory School

HANDBAG CONTENTS

Lipstick,
Perfume,
Coins and dust,
Purse,
Pencil,
Diary and dates a must!
Licence,
Car keys,
Odd hair clips,
Scissors,
Pens,
Sheets and slips.
Bus pass,
Notebook,
Photo frame,
All these things
What a pain!

Amy Holmwood (11)
Notre Dame Preparatory School

MONSTERS

Monsters are big,
Monsters are small,
Monsters are short,
And monsters are tall.
Monsters are good,
Monsters are bad
They're purple and green
And get really mad!

Abigail Baxter (9)
Notre Dame Preparatory School

ANIMALS

Animals are fast,
Animals are slow
Big, small, huge, tiny
Animals are funny,
Like a baby bunny.

Animals swim,
Animals jump,
Like a tiny fish
Like a bouncy
Kangaroo.
Jumping and hopping
As strong as can be,
But here comes the
Joey, trouble you can see.

Fish swimming under the sea,
Dogs and cats live on the land
You see.
Insects live in a jungle, maybe even a bee.
There's all kinds of animals that live on the land and the sea.
Animals eat meat and plants
They're God's creatures, always.

Alexander Kelly (9)
Notre Dame Preparatory School

MY CAT

I had a cat called Fluffball
She's very soft and warm
I cuddle her every day
I spoil her at dawn.

I love to give her treats
I stroke her soft head
She play fights with her brother
Then I send her to bed.

Amelia Cheeseman (8)
Notre Dame Preparatory School

2001

It's the new year
A year on from 2000
Fireworks and lights
Full of delights!

Soon January is over
It's February now
On 26th February
Dad's birthday is here!

I'm getting Dad a
Chris Tarrant's Millionaire Game.
So he can win and
For all of us to play.

On 1st March
It's my birthday
It hasn't come yet
So I wonder what I'll get?

I'm dreaming of a micro-scooter
A party, maybe more!
A bag full of pressies
From my pals and family.

Katrina Chia (9)
Notre Dame Preparatory School

CHRISTMAS

It's Christmastime!
Children singing carols and rhymes
Presents in their wrappings,
Stockings hanging on the wall.

At Christmastime
On the Christmas tree
There are chocolates just for me
And little parcels
Just for you.

It's bedtime
But no need to be sad
Tomorrow is Boxing Day
And I really should be glad
Because my auntie and uncle
Are coming to stay.

I feel like going 'whee'
Because we're going to have
A lovely tea!

Joseph Malpas (9)
Notre Dame Preparatory School

SNOW

In the snow the children play,
Throwing snowballs as cars drive away.
Snowmen waiting for their heads to come,
Without our gloves our fingers go numb.

Sliding down the hill we race,
It's hard to do up your lace.
Birds can't fly with frozen wings,
The town clock starts its winter rings.

People cheer that good old winter's here,
Wind whistling is the music we hear
It's a happy place in the frosty town
When Old King Winter has got his crown.

Maxwell Higgins (10)
Notre Dame Preparatory School

ROBOTS

Robots do everything for us
I mean they answer our phones
And play our CDs
We just sit back and relax
In 3000 there will be robots
Washing up, cleaning up,
Doing our homework!
Well that would be nice!

It's not like the good old days
When we did everything
Now these things
Have taken over, doing
Anything we want saying
'What you want, oh master?'

Some robots are good
A robot teacher 'No'
'A detention, dention.' 'Boom!'
'Yeah!' I shouted, my teacher
Had blown up!

So robots are alright but what
Will it be like in the year 3000
I wonder?

Jenna Slaughter (10)
Notre Dame Preparatory School

TIME

It ticks away
Every day
Morning, night
Dark and light
Through death and life
For a husband and wife
A daughter and son
The big moon and yellow sun
And the animals and fish.
For time is just a big round dish,
Going on forever
Until it stops forever
Then the poor old world will die
And just be a lonely planet in the sky.

Bryony Stanley (10)
Notre Dame Preparatory School

GIANT BEN

He is a big, big, fat, four-legged, dog
He eats anything and
He tramples over mountains
But when he gets to the top he
Just falls off.

He fell to a town
So they looked after him
He made friends with them
He protected them
From all other animals
They had a long friendship
Until he died.

Edward McNally (9)
Notre Dame Preparatory School

2002

Into the future
The next year on
Will there be monsters
In 2002?

Into the future
Wondering where to,
Whether there are robots
Can I take one home?

In the future where will I go
On holiday, under the ocean
Under the sea.

Up on the moon
I might go cycling on the
Moon's bumps.
It might be like quick sand.
It might not.

Harriet Steggles (9)
Notre Dame Preparatory School

SNOW

It's Christmastime and off we go
Off to the mountains full of snow
We're off to ski and have some fun
This year I'll try a black run
Sometimes it's foggy or bright
The snow can be fluffy or white
If the clouds come down you really can't see
Believe me it's true it happened to me.

Lucinda Steggles (11)
Notre Dame Preparatory School

HALLOWE'EN

It's Hallowe'en, it's Hallowe'en
It's Hallowe'en, it's Hallowe'en.
Where scary things jump out at night,
Who give you a sickening fright!
So in your dreams you might find
Something scary in your mind.
Like witches, ghouls, bats and fools,
Who scare you right out of your pants.

It's Hallowe'en, it's Hallowe'en
So try not to be scared it's only a dream
These things won't come true between you and me
But don't think these things are real
Because I'm a ghost and I'm pretty real
I'll give you a horrible fright
Ah, ha, ha, ha, ha!

Harry Millbank (10)
Notre Dame Preparatory School

MY BED

I love my bed
It is bright red
It's very comfy
And not too lumpy.

It's cosy at night
When I turn out the light
I snuggle down
And think of a clown.

I fall asleep
With dreams to keep
And wake in the morning
When the sun is dawning.

Under the cover
I hear my mother
Shout 'Get up please'
Oh no I'll freeze.

Emily Baxter (10)
Notre Dame Preparatory School

THE THINGS I LIKE

I like freshly cut
Grass.
I like roses in my back
Garden.
I like all my cuddly
Toys.
I like my hot water
Bottle on a cold night.
I like all my friends.
I like going to birthday parties.
I like big presents and
Small presents.
I like climbing trees.
I like going on my
Computer.
I like writing poems.

Bethany Richards (9)
Notre Dame Preparatory School

MY GARDEN

I walk through my garden what can I see?
A beautiful, orange honeybee,
The river full of fish
And the tree house . . . I wish.

As I walk down the path
To the mossy old bath
I see a robin in his nest,
With his family . . . and the rest.

I clamber through trees,
And spot a few rusty old keys,
With thorns in my fingers
And blood that lingers
A door is right ahead.

I see a hole for the key . . .
What a wonderful garden no one must see!

Emma Lusher (10)
Notre Dame Preparatory School

MY DRAGON

I have a dragon
His name is Ted
He is green and red
And he sleeps under my bed.

I feed him mice
All juicy and sliced
He thinks they're very nice
When eaten with rice.

He's very scaly
And sleeps like a baby
He thinks that maybe
I'm a special lady.

Meike Yallop (11)
Notre Dame Preparatory School

MY FAVOURITE ANIMAL

See if you can guess,
My favourite pet,
I will give you clues,
To help you choose.

It is pure clear white,
It comes out at night,
It is quick and,
Kind to you.

It is lazy in the day,
Feel sorry for rabbits,
And tiny mice and
Small Syrian hamsters.

It is ginger sometimes,
Brown or black,
It has short or long fur,
Silky, shiny, soft fur.

I have a friend,
Who has the same name,
We all call her Kat,
My pet is a cat.

Georgia Levell (10)
Notre Dame Preparatory School

DADS

Dads are funny, dads are cool
Some of them play the fool.
Some are PC
Pretty childish just like me
Some embarrass you
But in your homework they give you a clue.

Sometimes they're nasty and sometimes nice
It's so embarrassing when they look for the cheapest price
Dads, dads, dads I don't know where they get it from
I don't think it's grandad Tom.

When my friends come for tea
Dad treats them like they're only three
I can't complain really
When they come from work they are rather dreary.

But all in all we love them really
Although we see they're silly quite clearly.

Hollie Carter (9)
Notre Dame Preparatory School

FRIENDS

Anne-Marie, sweet as can be,
Bethany, good company,
Sabrina, Emma, Abigail too!
Are just some of my friends
How about you?

Chloe Bulpett (9)
Notre Dame Preparatory School

A PET RABBIT

Long-eared twitchy-nosed friend
Brown or spotty
Black or white
Cuddly, soft and furry thing.

A cabbage, carrot, lettuce too
Eating at its pleasure,
Rabbit mix, munch, munch, munch,
A rabbit cleaning afterwards.

Sweet and furry, cuddly thing
Soft and warm
A lovely, lovely bunny.

Rosie Thomas (8)
Notre Dame Preparatory School

JACKIE CHAN

I really like Jackie Chan
I am his favourite fan
He does complicated tricks
Like high flying kicks.

His stunts are amazing
He leaves the film directors gazing
His dad taught him to fight
And he fights with all his might.

His moves are really fast
He was in the Peking Theatre in the past.

Samuel Tawn (11)
Notre Dame Preparatory School

RIVERS

Rivers are flowing
Flowing gently
Fish are swimming around
In the bottom of the river
Reeds are swirling, swaying and rustling
In the wind.

The water is sparkling in the sunlight
Pebbles are rolling along the bank
Rolling deep under water
Mud is turning in the depths
Of the water.

I really like rivers
Peaceful, bubbling
Tumbling and graceful.

Rebecca Thouless (10)
Notre Dame Preparatory School

SILVER GOOSE

I thought I saw a silver goose
Glide across the sky
All the stars were its chicks
And the moon its nest.

The silver goose came up to me
I jumped onto its back
The silver goose took me on a flight
I will never forget
When I woke up
I found a silver feather!

Sabrina Johnson (9)
Notre Dame Preparatory School

WEATHER

Winter can be grey sometimes,
Or sunny
In England it's always cold
Especially in January.

In Scotland it snows
Very heavily
Floods are putting people in misery
People out of their houses.

In the summer it's boiling hot
But in winter it's definitely not
In winter you can throw snowballs
In summer you can go to the beach.

Matthew Adlard (9)
Notre Dame Preparatory School

DULL SUBJECTS

I hate maths at school
I can't do two plus two
Loathe all English
And grammar.

Science, I don't like to do,
Geography, I think it's boo
History, I could yell yucky
I think technology is mucky.

Like I said, I hate grammar
And spelling
Then why am I writing this smelly
poem?

Matilda Fitzmaurice (9)
Notre Dame Preparatory School

BUTTERFLIES

Look at the beautiful butterflies
The patterns are so neat
They fly around in the heat
On a beautiful summer's day.

Look at the beautiful butterflies
They fly from flower to flower
Taking all the nectar power
On a beautiful summer's day.

Look at the beautiful butterflies
Their colours are so bright
But they will have disappeared by night
On a beautiful summer's day.

Roxanne Mitchell (11)
Notre Dame Preparatory School

MY PET

My pet spends its time lying around
Doesn't do much
Just lies on the ground
She watches birds
Flying around
Has a very easy life.

My pet has four paws
Mostly likes milk
Sometimes plays with balls
She doesn't like dogs
Because they chase her in the kitchen.

My pet is a cat!

Harriet Kefford (9)
Notre Dame Preparatory School

HOME, HOME, HOME

A letter came through my door,
It said, you're in the war,
I said this is really cool,
And went and got my uniform.
When I got there I realised what war is,
My friends were being killed all around me
I wished I was at home, home, home,
My feet were so cold
They were like ice,
The bombs were falling all around me,
I was so scared,
I wondered if I was next to go over the top
I wish I was at home, home, home.
I was next,
I was the most scared I had ever been,
I went over,
I ran and fired my gun and then I realised
My legs had gone and I was down,
Never to see home, home, home again.

Emma Rust (12)
St Mary's VC Middle School, Long Stratton

THE WAVE

I was sitting on a wave one day.
When I met a fish called Kay.
He said 'Hello and how are you?'
I said to him 'How do you do?'

Emma Helliwell (9)
St Mary's VC Middle School, Long Stratton

PLAYTIME

People shouting, people running, children are jumping everywhere
Boys punching, boys crying, girls hopping, girls are skipping in the air.
Children pushing in the playground,
People falling over on the battleground.

Christopher Bartram (9)
St Mary's VC Middle School, Long Stratton

LUNCH TIME TERROR

Children crunching, children munching,
Lunch time is the worst
Boys are squabbling, girls are talking,
Dinner ladies everywhere
Teachers eating lunch, munch, munch, munch,
Dinner time terror starts at lunch
Punching is outlawed.

Samantha Jackson (9)
St Mary's VC Middle School, Long Stratton

SCISSORS

I have sharp, pointy blades
And my loops look like shades
Come and have a look at me
I'm the best scissors you will see.

Clip, clip the scissors cut your hair
Then it begins to give you a scare
Before too long your hair will shrink
And one or two will give you a wink.

Amy Jenkins (10)
St Mary's VC Middle School, Long Stratton

LUNCHTIME MAYHEM

Children munching, children crunching,
Lunchtime is so noisy
Chairs scraping, tables banging
Lunchtime is so noisy
Children pushing, children shoving,
Lunchtime is so noisy,
Plates sliding, knives scraping,
Lunchtime is so noisy!

Laura Brock (8)
St Mary's VC Middle School, Long Stratton

SCHOOL

Dinner lady shouting, wait.
    It's not your turn.
        Kicking, shoving in the line,
            Sam said 'That hurt.'
                Pushing, poking in the line.
                    Sally said 'You're no friend of mine.'
                    That's just our lunchtime.

Natalie Johnson (8)
St Mary's VC Middle School, Long Stratton

DINNER TIME

Shoving in the line,
Mr Blake yelling.
More nudging in the line,
Dinner ladies shrilling.
Children hollering,
Whilst others are calmly eating.

Charlotte Cutting (8)
St Mary's VC Middle School, Long Stratton

DINING HALL

People yelling, yelling, yelling,
Doors slamming, slamming, slamming,
Tables rattling, rattling, rattling,
Children pushing, pushing, pushing,
Chairs scrapping, scrapping, scrapping,
Tills clanging, clanging, clanging,
Money jingling, jingling, jingling,
Mr Blake shouting, shouting, shouting,
Boys and girls standing silently, still, still, still,
The sound of munching, munching, munching,
It's dinner time.

Carmen Lunness (8)
St Mary's VC Middle School, Long Stratton

VICKI

Vicki is my best friend,
Our friendship will never end,
She has golden, silk hair,
Her favourite animal is a bear,
She has glowing red lips,
Vicki likes cheese and onion chips,
She is my perfect friend,
Our friendship will never end,
She likes bright buttercup yellow,
Her sister plays a cello,
Vicki's a friend,
She lives down the road at the end!

Desiree Peeters (9)
St Mary's VC Middle School, Long Stratton

THE SEASONS

Spring is when the birds all sing and when a dove flaps
                                            its feathery wings.

Summer is when it's really sunny and when you see a little bunny.

Autumn is when the leaves all fall and the trees stand bare and tall.

Winter is when snowballs are thrown and when it hits the person
                                            will groan.

Alexander Henson (9)
St Mary's VC Middle School, Long Stratton

THE FRUIT MACHINE

The fruit machine stares you in the face
Then your mind starts to race
It winks a hundred hungry winks
Before you know your money sinks.

The fruit machine says pull the lever
All you know I might be a retriever
To the money I have stashed inside me
Some money'll come out, wait and see.

At first I beckoned you over to gamble your money
It'll be funny if you don't get it right
Come back again to me tonight.

Kimberley Stubbs (10)
St Mary's VC Middle School, Long Stratton

AFTER THE BELL

Off goes the buzzer
There go the children
Grab your lunch box
And off we go.

Push, shove in the queue
Me here, me there,
The doors fly open
And in we go.

In the dinner hall
What have you got?
I've got ham
She's got jam.
Chomp! Chomp! We go!

Jordanne Moy (9)
St Mary's VC Middle School, Long Stratton

IN THE HALL

Buzzer blasts, lunchtime starts
Boys slurping, children rushing
Girls moaning,
People eating everywhere.

Paige Bloomfield (9)
St Mary's VC Middle School, Long Stratton

BUMPS AND BRUISES

The playtime bell goes. Yippee!
Yes, at last we're all set free.

Jumping, running let's play catch
The boys just want a football match.

Bumps and bruises
Winners and losers.

We're making such a row
'Boys get out the toilets now!'

Ross Youngman (9)
St Mary's VC Middle School, Long Stratton

HALL AT LUNCHTIME

Here comes the children rushing in from play,
Here comes the teacher hip, hip hooray,
Hot lunch, packed lunch all around,
Discussing what they should do on the playground.

Standing in the queue,
Waiting for fun,
Pushing and shoving everyone.

Everyone thinks lunchtime is boring,
So everyone drops off snoring.

Rebecca Smith (9)
St Mary's VC Middle School, Long Stratton

THE SEA AND THE SAND

The sea was like a bottle of ink spilled over a sheet of white paper,
Fish like golden coins dropped in a wishing well.
Pieces of old stretched string that is used to tie down an old brown
                                        creaky boat float in the water.
Stones clatter at the bottom as the dolphins jump above.
Holiday makers chatter while crabs scuttle by to their rocky pool
                                        in the sand,
Rocks fall from the cliffs onto the boats which bob up and down
                                        in the light of the sun.
The sharks chase away the seals and tiny fish, the multicoloured
    seahorses and small creatures munch away at the nearby plants.
The golden sand gleams as little children play ball.

Safron Facey (9)
St John's Community Primary School, Hoveton

FAMILIES

First we'll start with mothers,
They shout at all the others!

        Second comes free with money,
        It's fathers all sweet as honey!

Third it turns out it's the sister,
To me she's just a huge great blister!

        Last and always least,
        Oh no it's the brother,
        Worse than any other.

All these things I said about you,
Were true,
But I shouldn't have said them!

Anna Ackroyd (9)
St John's Community Primary School, Hoveton

MY PET DOG

I have a pet dog called Bronte,
She acts like a donkey,
Yesterday she crashed into a tree,
Then she was scared by a flea,
Sometimes she's very mean,
But sometimes she's as happy as a bean,
When she was lively she chased after a mole,
But then she got her head stuck in a rabbit's hole,
One day on Salhouse Broad she jumped into a muddy lake
And she came out like a pitch-black snake,
We always have to tell her to heal,
Because she always pulls me down the field,
She's as fast as a cheetah,
So we call her the Defeater,
I'll never say she is a pest,
Because she is just the best!

Emma Brook (9)
St John's Community Primary School, Hoveton

MY CAT

At night my cat creeps along in the mist, like a fox,
My cat is very cute like a baby rabbit,
Hello, my cat says as she goes in and out,
She caught a mouse, argh!
At night as the moon comes out she purrs,
Next morning I pour her some milk,
Drip, drip,
She jumps like a ball,
She snouts around,
I love my little cat.

Stacey Edwards (9)
St John's Community Primary School, Hoveton

IN MY FAMILY

In my family there's me, Emily the fussy one.
My sister Louise, she's nice,
But the only good thing about older sisters
Are they give you their old things, (hint, hint).
My little brother William
You don't want to know about him,
All I can tell you is don't have a brother.
Then of course there's my mum
Always telling me what to do.
My dad is just the same, always going on.
My dog's name is Jenny, she is the sweetest in the world.
Folly and Max, the rabbits,
Folly too ginger and Max too black
Taz is just lovely, just ginger and black,
So he makes a Max and a Folly
I'll shut the door and I'll say . . .
I'm so glad you came, bye for now, see ya again!

Emily Linnell (10)
St John's Community Primary School, Hoveton

THE DREAM OF THE BEAR

Under the moon, comet and stars,
There is the bear,
Brown fur, gold eyes,
He is waiting for me.

Me in my white gown,
Floats to the cloud where the bear is waiting,
Brown fur, gold eyes,
He is there on the cloud.

I dance till dawn,
On the cloud so soft on my feet,
I float to my window,
Get into bed and go to sleep.

Under the moon, comet and stars,
There is the bear,
Brown fur, gold eyes,
He is waiting for me.

Amber Press (10)
St John's Community Primary School, Hoveton

RUN, RUN

Amber and me orienteering,
Jumping through the pond,
Slashing, sploshing, peering, jeering,
Sinking in the mud,
Run, run,
I can't shout for Mum,
There's a pike over there,
I really don't care,
I've got duckweed in my hair,
So for heaven sakes run,

I wish I was in my bed,
But instead I'm nearly dead,
And I'm going a bit red,
And I just want to cuddle my ted,
We climbed out the pond,
Not cool, like James Bond,
So we ran all the way home,
All on our own.

Katrin Whitten (9)
St John's Community Primary School, Hoveton

MY SISTER

My sister can be quite annoying
And bossy too.
She is quite perfect
And beautiful and doesn't care about you.
She is eight years old,
And comes from the planet Mars.
She's fun to play with
But eats all the chocolate bars.
She can't play darts,
But she can break metal bars.
She sucks up to everyone
Especially me
She doesn't care if she is fat or not
But she is my sister
And I love her . . . not!

Amy Ledgerwood (9)
St John's Community Primary School, Hoveton

MY CAT

My cat's fluffy with a big black nose
She is a little terror and I know it so,
I touch her tummy and she scratches me
She goes outside for an hour or three,
My cat brings back lots of dead mice.
And comes to wake me in the middle of the night.
My mum goes to work at five in the morning
The cat goes out when the rain is pouring,
I go downstairs and open the door
And there is my cat soaking wet on the floor.

Peter Jones (9)
St John's Community Primary School, Hoveton

MY BEDROOM

My bedroom's a dump,
My bedroom's a tip,
I really must clean it up and get a grip,
The carpet's full of sweet wrappers, there's cobwebs everywhere
It took nearly a month to find some clean underwear.
I woke up in the morning and wonder where I am
Urgg I just remembered it's that rotting piece of ham!
I once had a dream, my bedroom was nice and clean
My radio was playing Robbie Williams' Love Supreme
Looking at my bedroom now I know this will never be
But still it's my bedroom and my bedroom will always be me.

Gareth Lewis (10)
St John's Community Primary School, Hoveton

MY HAMSTER

He runs around his cage with a little bare tail
He often runs and thinks he's part of Willy Whale.
I open the cage door,
And he runs onto the floor,
He slips and slides onto the chair,
But don't worry he doesn't care,
Then disaster my mum shouts tea,
No Midget please don't do a wee,
I grab a sponge to clear it up
And oh dear I broke a cup.
I better run or I'll be late,
I know my mum she gets in a state.

Belinda Lodge (10)
St John's Community Primary School, Hoveton

MY BEDROOM

My bedroom is a pig sty,
My bedroom is a pest
I can't see the floor
It's covered in mess,
'Tidy your room.'
Came a shout up the stairs,
'Clear up those toys.'
So I picked up my bears,
But who really cares,
I put them away on my bed
I'll put my clothes in my wardrobe
Downstairs I'll hang
My bathrobe,
I'll put my toys under my bed,
I went downstairs to have my tea,
Then I ended up watching TV.

Aisha Cook (9)
St John's Community Primary School, Hoveton

ROBOTS

I made a robot,
Wheels of wood,
Body of steel,
Scary face,
Flick up spike,
To stop the enemy,
Remote controlled,
Lever action,
To tip up opponent.

Jamie Boddington (9)
St John's Community Primary School, Hoveton

SPACE

I once went into space,
And never left a trace,
I went before my bath time,
And I know this won't rhyme,
But I hate baths a lot.

I found a cardboard box
But I had the chickenpox
So I took some cream just in case
I pushed a lever and I started to go
Up the chimney and away we go.

Space was lovely with the twinkling stars,
But the aliens laughed when they saw my car,
The planets were red with blue and purple spots
Asteroids came down in lots and lots.

I came to a halt when I heard my mum
It's bath time dear now, please don't run
So I wondered upstairs in a big, big strop
And as I got right up to the top
Into the bathroom I fell with a drop.

After my bath I climbed into bed,
And pulled the covers over my head,
I turned off the light
And dreamt of the adventures
I'd had that night.

Amy Clarke (10)
St John's Community Primary School, Hoveton

THE VALENTINE

One misty evening
In the moonlight.
I saw a boy and girl
In the moonlight.

They met by the lake
In the moonlight.
He gave her a diamond
In the moonlight.

She dropped the ring in the lake
In the moonlight.
He dived in and retrieved it
In the moonlight.

She gave him a letter
In the moonlight.
It said meet me at ten
In the moonlight.

He came back the next evening
In the moonlight.
They kissed
In the moonlight.

Then they ran away
In the moonlight.

Luke Cook (10)
St John's Community Primary School, Hoveton

MY SONG

Michael, Michael that's my name
I am the champion of this game,
I love the colour red
It's the colour of my bed,
I've got a friend called Jack, he likes pool and he's cool,
My mum's a nurse and once I took a tenner out of her purse,
My mum went mad
And called me a bad lad.
My teacher gave me a sum
I got it wrong and I got smacked on my bum!
When I got back from school I had a game of pool
But my mum shouted 'Come get some pie.'
So I have to say 'Bye, bye.'

Michael Sommerfield (9)
St John's Community Primary School, Hoveton

DAY POEM

The sun like a new penny shines,
Laughter from children echoes,
Clouds like candyfloss float by,
Cars stay in their drives and people walk,
Men and women lay on beaches while children splash in the sea,
People sit in offices gazing at computer screens,
Delivering drivers drive round in circles searching for houses,
Train drivers take families to the sea,
Then the sun began to drop and the darkness dominates the sky.

Daniel Chaney (10)
St John's Community Primary School, Hoveton

MY BROTHERS

My brothers I can't quite explain
They are both different people
Oh I forgot, their names are
Lewis and Ben.
My brother's teeth are green and black
All over Ben's room are sweaty clothes
'Don't go in there!'
You can't find your way in and
You can't find your way out.
So we don't go in there
Lewis' room is like PC World
It is a stink bomb
At the end of the day
They're my brothers and boys
Will be boys.

Bethany Moore (9)
St John's Community Primary School, Hoveton

MY COUSIN

I have a little cousin his name is Charlie George
He is a little terror but I love him very much,
He pulls out your hair and he pinches your nose,
He lives in a small house where he continually grows.
He scares the ducks down at the pond,
And of the horses he is very fond,
He does not like bath time he always splashes,
When on his own his bedroom he trashes
But I still love my cousin very much!

Emily Moore (9)
St John's Community Primary School, Hoveton

ALIENS

I've got some friends who are aliens,
They look very funny,
But I don't mind,
For inside they're just like me.

One is orange with pink polka dots,
He's got three eyes,
And he smells a lot!

Another alien friend who I call Fred,
Has got four arms,
And a big purple head!

I've got a girlfriend alien as well,
I sent her a Valentine card,
And she said it was swell!

One is very greedy,
She's got a big fat tummy,
And her name is Deedee!

Everyone laughs at my friends,
But I don't mind,
For inside they're just like me!

Rachael Oakley (10)
St John's Community Primary School, Hoveton

WHAT IS A STORM?

The storm is like guns banging on a battlefield.
It is like the inside of a vacuum cleaner.
It is like a dripping tap, that won't stop.
It is like a cracked plate.

Craig Bassam (8)
St John's Community Primary School, Hoveton

THE WINTER MONTH

Snowflakes falling like white confetti in
The cold, cold sky of the winter earth,
Icicles are like wind chimes blowing in the breeze.

An abandoned fire flickering like water ripples in the sea,
Trees are bare like a poor old man reaching for a penny,
Christmas waste scattered in the city.

The year is coming to an end like a university student,
Holly like green velvet pin cushion,
Robin's red breast is like sections of a raspberry.

Children build a snowman shivering at the touch.

Olexandra Solomka (9)
St John's Community Primary School, Hoveton

WF

Stone Cold's got passion,
He does his stuns with fashion.
The Rock is very strong,
He has a great song.
Kurt Angle always has a cheat,
For a holiday he goes to Crete.
Triple H gets the pedigree
And then he always gets one, two, three.
The Undertaker's pretty lethal,
Then he acts evil.
The Dudley Boys always get the 3D
But sometimes they can get free.
Stephanie slaps really hard,
So Trish's face looks scarred.

Brett Jenner (10)
St John's Community Primary School, Hoveton

MY DOG

My dog is a golden retriever,
When we walk he crouches down
He gets scared when we get to a lamp post,
He barks when there is nobody there
My dog is jumping up on two legs
My dog gets out of the shed,
My dog gets muddy on the grass,
We wash him outside with shampoo.

Paul Arundel (9)
St John's Community Primary School, Hoveton

THE WHALE

One day at the sea
There was a whale in the water.
In the dirty sea,
It smelt horrible,
It looked scary,
It looked black, dark and white,
In the sea.

Beth Aldridge (8)
St John's Community Primary School, Hoveton

THERE WAS AN OLD MAN FROM SPAIN

There was an old man from Spain,
Who tried to throw his wife down the drain,
She kicked him in the head,
And he turned all red,
And she said my real name's Elaine.

Jack Stuttle (10)
St John's Community Primary School, Hoveton

THE END OF THE WORLD

One day in 10000
There was a man
Who could drive a van
He was going round the town.

Then he saw a fire ball
He went as fast as he could
To go to the alarm and set it off
The people ignored the alarm.

They thought it was a practice
But then they saw it
In five seconds *boom!*
That was the end of the world.

Peter Morley (9)
St John's Community Primary School, Hoveton

WHAT IS THE SKY?

The sky is a blue piece of paper,
With glue on it.

It is a blue box,
With white paper inside.

It is a navy shirt,
With white paint down it.

It is a pale blue bag,
With tiny tears.

It is an English book,
With pieces of a broken ruler.

Amy Platten (8)
St John's Community Primary School, Hoveton

To Make My Robot

To make my robot I will . . .
Push in some wheelchair motors,
Place in some wires and a spare fan
My weapons will be a strong and powerful pickaxe.
A ramming spike and a flipper and maybe a scoop,
I want to destroy that Chaos Two,
I want to be a Robot Wars Champion,
I will batter and wrench on Robot Wars
I have reached the semi-final,
I am against my worst nightmare Hypnodisk (indestructible robot)
But you humans are wrong, I will win!

Darren Firman (9)
St John's Community Primary School, Hoveton

My Boat

My boat is speedy,
It goes like a rocket over the waves
It comes and goes all over the place
You can hear the engine coming over the sea
What is it?
A plane?
A ship?
No! It is my boat
A nineteen metre boat
The sound of the pumps, pumping petrol
It is white and blue
It goes like new
Then its last voyage around the world.

Christopher Morcher (9)
St John's Community Primary School, Hoveton

THE OGRE FROM OXFORD

The ogre from Oxford is slimy
And definitely ugly
It is hairy
And definitely deadly.

The ogre from Oxford is foul,
And definitely vicious
It is fetid,
And definitely monstrous.

The ogre from Oxford is horrible,
And definitely mouldy
It is so smelly
And definitely bold.

The ogre from Oxford is tall,
And definitely stinky
It is so cold
And definitely bumpy.

. . . That's the ogre from Oxford!

Bradley Starkings (9)
St John's Community Primary School, Hoveton

WHAT IS A DESERT ISLAND?

A desert island is a green ball rolling on blue paper.
It is a lizard resting on dry sand.
It is a mist of tropical colours blurred in a background of green.
It is green stripes, brown, then all just dust.
It is the sun, splashing on the sea.
It is a blur of different greens mixed together in a bowl of yellow.
It is a blur of silent nothingness.

Zoe Howard (9)
St John's Community Primary School, Hoveton

WHAT IS THE SKY?

The sky is blue like the sea but higher than it would be.

It is like the movies but high up in the air.

It is like a puddle high up in the air so far away.

It is old white cotton wool floating high up in the air.

It is white and blue paper high up in the air.

That's what the sky is.

Natalie Morton (8)
St John's Community Primary School, Hoveton

IF THE WORLD WAS TO END

If the world was to end
I wouldn't have a friend.

If the world was to die
There wouldn't be you or I.

If the world was to stop
There wouldn't be a drop of rain.

If the world was to close
No rivers would flow.

But if the world was to stay
We could play and treasure each day.

James Walpole (9)
St John's Community Primary School, Hoveton

WHAT IS A STORM?

The storm is a load of cotton wool dyed grey and blown away up high.
It is a large drum kit being banged so loudly it rumbles around the
Earth.
It is hundreds of rotten candyfloss in a dark cupboard.
It is lots of feathers stuck together with a torch shining through.
It is a powerful bird that flies around the Earth.

Joshua Cook (9)
St John's Community Primary School, Hoveton

SAND SLASH

Sand Slash smelly and fat
With a spiky head
Mind he does not get you
If he does he will eat your bones
Use your teeth as necklaces
Your eyes as gobstoppers
Cut your toes off, then your fingers
And then he will feed them to his dog who likes to eat bones!

Jamie Archer (8)
St John's Community Primary School, Hoveton

THE STORM

The storm is a piece of thunder going through
A dark, dark frightening sky.
A storm is when a gust of wind comes at you from
The dark, dark frightening sky
The storm is like blue paint coming down from the sky.

Thomas Desborough (8)
St John's Community Primary School, Hoveton

WHAT IS A STORM?

A storm is when the wind screams at you.
When places are wrecked.
When roofs come off houses.
When windows are smashed.
When people die.
When trees start to snap.
When animals begin to die.
When doors are broken.
When schools are broken into.

Nicholas Simons (8)
St John's Community Primary School, Hoveton

WHAT IS A TORNADO?

The tornado is like dirty water going down the plug hole.
It is someone stirring melted chocolate.
It is like a car wash spinning quickly.
It is like dust coming off a fast car.
It is someone wiping the windows quickly in circles.

Matthew Varley (8)
St John's Community Primary School, Hoveton

WHAT IS THE SEA?

The sea is salt dropped into water,
It is water at a beach with sand.
It is a lace where we can yacht.
It is like a blue ruler that has been dropped into the sea.
It is like a blue pencil case that has be dropped into the sea.

Mikey Ward (8)
St John's Community Primary School, Hoveton

A Tornado

The tornado is twisting through the rainy storm
It's whizzing away
All of the cars had their windows smashed
The people were frightened about the tornado.

The tornado smashed their houses in half
The people were upset
They had nowhere to live anymore.

Daniel Outing (8)
St John's Community Primary School, Hoveton

The Grinch

The Grinch has two big eyes,
He smells like an unflushed toilet,
More disgusting than a dirty rubbish bin,
Uglier than the ugliest man on Blind Date,
Hairier than a gorilla,
Fatter than the fattest pig in the world,
Mouldier than sandwiches left in a bag for two weeks,
Slimier than a plumber down a drain,
Dirtier than a pig farmer when he comes home from work.

Rose-Marie Cooke (9)
St John's Community Primary School, Hoveton

How To Build A Robot

I shall start with the engine and I'll put it in there
I shall get the wheels and stick on there,
I shall push and pull until they fit,
I shall add some diesel to make it fast,
I shall put in wires and add some nuts,
I shall join up the wires to make it run.
I shall pop on the cover to make it done.
Oh no it's broken!

Sebastian Waters (9)
St John's Community Primary School, Hoveton

I Hate School

I hate school we have to look smart.
I like school I play my part.
I hate school we aren't allowed to play anything good.
I like school I hit people round the head with wood.
I hate school I don't like writing.
I like school 'cause I like fighting.
I hate school I don't like science tests.
I like school 'cause I like all the rest.

Grant Sheppard (9)
St John's Community Primary School, Hoveton

MONSTERMOGENS

My monstermogen has a big, grizzly mouth,
He sometimes like to eat clouds,
And eat yummy people.

He likes chilli, he fiddles with people's stuff,
He's really mouldy and filthy,
And he's usually stinky!
He had for breakfast chilli on toast,
For afters he had people with chilli.

Kyle Oakley (9)
St John's Community Primary School, Hoveton

WHAT IS THE EARTH?

The Earth is a Brussel sprout frying in a pan.
It is like fingerprints on a dark sheet of paper.
It is a green and blue bouncy ball.
It is blue pond with green lily pads.
It is a small ball of green and blue sparks.
It is a blob of ink dropping onto some paper.
It is like a ball with splodges of paint.
It is like a rock bouncing about.

Lauren O'Brien (9)
St John's Community Primary School, Hoveton

WINTER

Hair-swoosher,
Field-whiter,
Air-chiller,
Ice-breaker,
Sky-frostier,
Play-slushier,
Window-sparkler,
Hail-blower,
Ice-freezer,
Sledge-spinner,
Body-shiverer,
Toe-tingler,
Eye-waterer,
Tree-singer,
Nose-runner,
Cheek-tingler,
Fingers-frozener.

Lucy Appleton (10)
Stoke Holy Cross Primary School

MRS O'GRADY

Mrs O'Grady is a bright, shiny red,
Also a warm summer day
And a school playground buzzing with children's voices
She is a gentle breeze on a hot day.
Mrs O'Grady is a pair of gardening jeans,
She is a jabbering television.
Mrs O'Grady is a gardening programme showing flowers of all kinds,
She is a tasty pancake.

Olga Turner (10)
Stoke Holy Cross Primary School

LONELINESS

All alone in the dark,
Not a sound stirs,
Listening carefully to your breath,
In the gloom no sound is heard,
Trying to hear a noise,
Any noise,
Waiting for someone to uncover you,
In the dark, no sound is heard,
How long have you been here?
You do not know,
You can't survive for much longer,
Need to get out
But how?
How can you?
Underneath the rubble and dirt,
No sound is heard.

Doug Appleby (10)
Stoke Holy Cross Primary School

TOTAL RUBBISH

It can be yellow,
Dropped by a fellow.
It can be a pan
Dropped by an old man.
It can be stinky
A reddy-pinky.
Now people are getting mad,
About people dropping rubbish which is bad
So keep our world clean and neat
Keep our world a lovely treat.

Alec Francis (9)
Stoke Holy Cross Primary School

MY GRANDAD

I remember when he laughed,
Spoke in a funny voice,
When he took his teeth out.
He had a great mind
Laughing when he thought something was funny.
When he laid on the hospital bed for the first time and the last time
He said
'My time has come, let me go.'
He was allowed to go home,
His mind went dead,
No laughter came out of him,
I felt alone,
Scared when he went,
No laughter anymore
In the house where he used to live,
Now only my nan lives there,
Frightened scared on her own,
Wants to see him again,
Wants him back again.
Seeing his grave brings memories back,
Daisies on his grave.

Jemma Bale (11)
Stoke Holy Cross Primary School

SPACE

Space, the black darkness of the infinite universe,
Space, with all its planets, sun, moon, stars and meteorites,
Space, the black holes that suck you in,
Space, the satellites and the rockets we send up there,
Space, the dangerous place.

Jonathan Millington (9)
Stoke Holy Cross Primary School

MY GRANDAD

My grandad is a 'gardeney' person,
He loves the smell of flowers,
He has a purply coloured cheek,
His birth mark
Poor him,
He must have been scared of operations.
He had lots,
I remember,
That bed
Where he lay after his heart attack,
People gave cards,
Flowers,
Presents,
He loved it.
I remember
When he came home
He sat
In his armchair.
I woke up at six
Every morning
I helped him get up
I fed him in the half term weeks
I did exercises with him
For six whole months
It was hard
It frightened me, seeing him like that,
I cried
I cried every night,
Then I couldn't help holding back my tears,
He knew how I felt,
He was upset too.

Melissa Knights (10)
Stoke Holy Cross Primary School

THE LION

The lion stalks about
Feared by all creatures
Brings terror where it walks
Stalks its prey like a stealth fighter in battle
Camouflaged in the towering grass which stretches to the
heavens above
Comes to rest in the shade and safety of a nearby tree
Hears the tour bus coming
Stands tall, strong and bold,
In his safe haven
Hears the click, click of cameras,
Children stand and point,
The lion stands there, allows himself to be photographed,
the bus drives on,
The bus is only a faint rumble in the distance
Hears gazelle's feet on the hard ground
Once again slinks into the towering grass,
Crawls creeps up to the gazelle
They sense something, ears pricked,
The lion stands still as a statue,
Gazelles think nothing of it, carry on grazing,
Suddenly the lion shows himself
Charges at the gazelles
Picks out the weakest, attacks,
Down comes the gazelle, sudden death,
Back the gazelle is dragged, back to the lion's tree,
Tonight they will feast on the daily kill.
This is my lion the bravest of them all
The one that rules the park,
And brings fear where it walks.

Alexander Abbott (11)
Stoke Holy Cross Primary School

ART

When I do art,
I think I'm smart,
Now let's start,
Let's draw Bart.
Paper and pen
I draw a hen
Scissors and paint,
I think I'll faint
Pencil crayons and felt pens
Let's draw doors for our ends.
Brushes and pots,
Let's make lots
Water and glue
I like blue.
Colours and wax,
Lucy likes Max.
When I do art
I really think I'm smart.

Rebecca Herdman (10)
Stoke Holy Cross Primary School

MY CAT

My cat was always friendly,
He was clever, he opened windows,
He petrified dogs, he crossed the road like a human,
He terrified old people,
He waited outside the pub.

Philip Dennis (10)
Stoke Holy Cross Primary School

MY HAMSTER

Always in that room,
How lonely you must get,
Shaking at the bars as if to say 'Let me out'
Running round your wheel making it squeak and squeal,
Always twitching every second of every minute,
Your whiskers long and pointy but also sensitive
You always look me in the eye
Just staring at me
Your golden fur gleaming in the midday sunlight,
I can see your little heart beating,
When I pick you up I feel your tiny bones
If only you could speak
What a story you would tell.

Alex Walmsley (10)
Stoke Holy Cross Primary School

A NIGHT ON THE EYE

As I look down from the London Eye
I see people walking by
The shop lights look like golden plates
Plastered on a black sea
The sound of taxi horns grows low as the night draws on,
And businessmen go home for tea
Big Ben chimes nine - shop lights go off
But the city is still stirring -
Clubs, bars,
Their lights are still on,
I'm at the bottom of the 'Eye' now
I just can't leave it
What an experience!

Nathan Wilson (9)
Stoke Holy Cross Primary School

My Uncle Charlie

I remember his long, thin, white face, laying so still on his hospital bed
I said 'You're not going to live very long'
A tear went down my hot cheek and more and more and more
I remember on New Year's Eve that night when he passed away
His wife auntie Peggy was in Australia but uncle Charlie had
                    Parkinson's Disease when he was twenty-one
He had lived for seventy-eight years and now he is in his grave with
                    some weeping violets by his side
But I will not forget about my uncle Charlie the kind,
                    warm-hearted man
I saved one hundred and fifty pounds for the
                    Parkinson's Disease Charity
He would never eat or ever drink or ever take his tablets that's why he
                    died on New Year's Eve night
I hope he rests in peace.

Emily Bird (10)
Stoke Holy Cross Primary School

Annie

Annie my only dog
Golden fur and sweet diamond eyes
I remember on Christmas Day
She ran playing in the snow
She sat in my group of teddies
She even looked like one, cute and fluffy
Loved to have company
She loved to play football, she always won
She was always happy
I got her on my birthday, she was very warm
But then we had to give her away
My heart will always be broken.

Daniel Mclean (11)
Stoke Holy Cross Primary School

DISNEYLAND PARIS

Happy sounds of children laughing with the characters
How colourful they look
Winnie the Pooh lollies that they took
Flashing colours all the time as you walk round
Feel the vibrations of the roller coaster as you walk along the ground
Candy hanging in the shops above your head
While you're there you wish it was never bed.
Watching fireworks as they enter the sky
In all the most extraordinary colours it certainly catches your eye.
Tall pointed buildings you enter and are amazed
Posters and pictures of the characters are always being gazed
You can go to the funfair ground
See entertainment all around
A squeak, a yell, it's there all the time
Whizz down, round, on the helter-skelter
Gliding through the air.

Sammy-Jo Smithson (10)
Stoke Holy Cross Primary School

THE BLUES

Bahamas-blue, aqua-blue,
Sea-blue, midnight-blue,
The deep blue sea,
The sky in summer,
The coldness of winter,
Icicles dripping,
Loneliness,
Sadness.

Susannah Gordon (9)
Stoke Holy Cross Primary School

MAGIC POTION

Hubble, hubble, this means trouble
Rain, burn and cauldron hubble.

Tail of scorpion, fur of dog,
Head of fish and guts of frog,
Buzzard beak and duck webbed feet,
Panda eye, cow with meat,
Breath of ant and monkey's ear,
Nose of tiger, horn of deer,
Feather of parrot, snail shell,
Toe of monkey, church's bell.

Hubble, hubble this means trouble
Rain, burn and cauldron, hubble.

Richie Leech (11)
Stoke Holy Cross Primary School

WORLD'S FUTURE

All the ways I can see,
In the future this may be,
Footballs square,
Rabbits beware,
No guns here or there,
In the future this may be too
See the world as clear as me,
But don't relax this can be,
No more wars here to see,
We must let everybody see
How grateful we can be
In years to come this can be.

Tom Kemp (10)
Stoke Holy Cross Primary School

WHAT MY CAT SPIKE DOES

When we got Spike he was a kitten
He had really big ears, but still he was cute
He was ginger like fire,
Had really sharp teeth
He likes to bite your legs
And likes to go to sleep.
When he grew up
He was really quite fat
He doesn't catch mice
Can you imagine that?
He plays outside to have some fun
And on a hot day he lies in the sun.
When he comes in he lies on my bed
He dreams, dreams in his head.

Rebecca Taitt (9)
Stoke Holy Cross Primary School

THE BIG SCARY HOUSE

This is about a scary big house
It's scary and spine-chilling
Nearly all wooden and dark,
Old and the floorboards creak
It rattles and it sounds
Like someone's screaming
You can hear someone whispering and whistling
Loads of mice on the stairs
You can hear someone knocking on the doors
There's lots of bats flying in the air
You should not go there
Ha, ha, ha!

Jacob Masters (9)
Stoke Holy Cross Primary School

DEAD WOOD

Thou has betrayed the King of Wood
Queen Titania thought you should
The king is angry bow down low,
You are evil, you must go;
Go and seek on yonder plain,
See who will accept your pain
Go and seek what you can see
But don't come back and plead to me
And if you ever see a tree
Thou should grovel, think of me;
If thee should ever tread this floor,
Thou should have a head no more;
So pack the things that ye doesn't own,
Walk away, you are alone;

Thou has betrayed the King of Wood.

Harrison Cooter (10)
Stoke Holy Cross Primary School

A RIDE OF THRILL

It twists and turns,
Jolts and jerks,
It's nail-biting stuff really,
You scream and yell,
As it zooms around,
You sway and swing,
When it loops the loop,
It whirls and twirls
And finally comes to a stop.

Joshua Harl (9)
Stoke Holy Cross Primary School

SOMEONE VERY SPECIAL

He has thundering hooves
That go clip, clop, clip, clop
He has a grey forelock, mane and tail
He has pointy ears that stick forward
He is a Lusutano Stallion,
His name is Confiardo.
You can see him well at night
He has a very speedy canter
I feed him every Sunday.
I muck out his stable every Sunday.
Confiardo likes to sniff
The new stables he goes in
He is a white horse
And I love him truly.
I wouldn't give him up
For any other horse.

Holly-May Barber (10)
Stoke Holy Cross Primary School

DESCRIBING A CHINCHILLA

They have big black eyes
At night they like to stare.
They have big bushy tails
That wave in the air.
They're cute, they are fluffy,
With big mouse ears,
They are joyful and trusting
And will treat you with care.

Annemarie Sewell (9)
Stoke Holy Cross Primary School

BATTY

I remember that she had big, fluffy fur,
When she was hungry she used to have big sad eyes,
She used to jump up on the bar then people would feed her,
She used to fish upon the river.

I remember one snowy day she got stuck up on a tree,
I was the one that got her,
She liked to watch the Planets Funniest Animals,
Once she went next door and stole their biggest fish.

I remember Batty liked to dance to my CDs
She always drank milk,
When I was laying on the floor reading she would jump on my back
And lean on my head to read with me.

Danny Sutton (11)
Stoke Holy Cross Primary School

MY FRIEND SAMANTHA

My friend Samantha has brown eyes,
She has brown hair,
We play together all the time,
I sit next to her at school.
If Samantha is upset I comfort her,
We share our secrets,
We see each other at Brownies,
We'll be friends forever.

Amber Moon (10)
Stoke Holy Cross Primary School

MY SECRET HIDING PLACE

I have a secret hiding place
Nobody knows where it is
I'll tell you if you promise not to tell
No one can see my secret hiding place
For it blends into its background
Can you guess where it is?
My secret hiding place sits as still as a statue
                              with dark and light bushes around it
In my secret hiding place I have a stack of books as tall as me
I have food and drink to last me a lifetime
It feels good to lie on the floor and stare at the cloudy sky
Now go to the apple tree, turn right, look around
And you will see a clump of bushes
That's where my hiding place is
So don't tell anyone
Sssshhh!

Jessica Withey (10)
Stoke Holy Cross Primary School

MY FRIEND TOM

My friend Tom has made me twice as good at football
He always says his things are better,
He loves coming round mine,
He's got blond hair and blue eyes,
He often gets annoyed with me,
And he really wants to be a footballer
But he would also like to be a popstar
He really likes coming on adventures on my dad's farm.

Robert King (10)
Stoke Holy Cross Primary School

HOLIDAY FUN

The snow was white
It came at night
The snow was fun
I did a black run
The bum boards were great
I stayed up very late
Ashley Ross' friend
Played with him till the end.
It was quite hot
I liked it a lot
My mum was quite good
Dad didn't' ski the way you should
Then we went to say
Thank you for our holiday!

Freya Warburton (9)
Stoke Holy Cross Primary School

PETS

A puppy is my favourite pet
They are so cute
Their noses are all cold and wet.
My worst pet is a newt
Because they are all slimy, they are green and covered in scales
I also love to see dolphins and whales
Dolphins and whales can never be a pet
I would love to swim with dolphins and whales.

Heidi Leech (8)
Stoke Holy Cross Primary School

SPACE

We're flying through space
The air is so clear
Keep your head inside or you might lose your ear!

The ship is nice and clean
So very, very clean
But all the aliens over there are very, very green!

There are so many buttons in this ship
I don't know what's what
And this one needs a new microchip!

It is so big outside in space
I don't know where we are
It is hard to see if anything is nearby or far!

Tristen Read (8)
Stoke Holy Cross Primary School

A CANDLE'S LIFE

Candle burning in the night,
Candle burning with all its might.
Bedroom glowing very bright,
Bedroom glowing can't be night.
Morning breaks so bright
Candle can't burn with all its might
Candle gone oh that's all right,
Candle gone out of sight
Candle will come back at night
Then it will glow with all its might.

Elin Holbeck (9)
Stoke Holy Cross Primary School

SWIMMING

Swimming is fun,
Swimming is hard,
I would love to be in the Olympics
I guess it is all a dream
But I hope one day it will come true
Or at least I will have been seen
Galas are hard you have to use your muscles
You have to try at least five times to be quite good anyway
You must not forget about the fun in swimming
Floats and handstands
Roly-polys are OK
Don't forget swimming lessons
They are not that bad, OK
Gold, silver and bronze medals are also all a dream,
But remember you have to try or you will not be seen.

Harriet Abbott (9)
Stoke Holy Cross Primary School

THE CORKSCREW

I felt my stomach churning as the roller coaster car clanked up the chain
Then I felt the wind roar in my face as I plummeted down
I felt my stomach fly out of my mouth as the car banked
We shot to the double loop
Then we hurtled towards the station platform
I stepped onto it with my hair on end.

Sam Hogden (9)
Stoke Holy Cross Primary School

TYPES OF WEATHER

Weather can be good,
Weather can be bad.
Weather can make you happy,
Weather can make you sad.
Weather like acid rain can hurt trees and leaves,
Then there is the gentle flowing breeze!
Rainbows are funny things, they come out after the rain, in the sun
Some people like to be out in the open sun,
While others prefer the shade, nice and dark and cold
Like those who are old
Weather, either sun or rain will still be the same unpredictable weather.

Alasdair Roat (8)
Stoke Holy Cross Primary School

DINOSAURS

Tyrannosaurus in the rain,
Pterodactyl is home again
Brachiosaurus very tall,
A Diplodocus could fill the hall.
A Velociraptor chasing me,
A Stagasaurus by the tree
A Triceratops in the sun
Barosaurs having fun
Deinonychus looking at a puddle of vomit,
Uh oh here comes a comet
Quickly run fast, fast, fast
There goes the dinosaurs at last.

Matt Beaumont (9)
Stoke Holy Cross Primary School

THE WILDERNESS

T ired tigers on fresh, green grass
H airy hippos bathing in the warm water
E lephants having a big, wet water fight.

W acky monkeys swing on trees
I ncredible red-bottomed baboons
L ions hunting for their prey
D aft deer running across the road
E agles swooping down to catch mice
R abbits bouncing higher and higher
N aughty hyenas teasing each other
E very animal in the wilderness is wild
S nakes are slithering on the green grass
S low turtles swimming in the sea.

Piers Goodwin (8)
Stoke Holy Cross Primary School

CROCODILE

The crocodile is so long and green that means he's very hard to be seen
When the animals come for a drink at the river
They all seem to start to quiver
I'm not quite sure why but I've heard some of them have died
Been eaten alive in pretty much all in a writhe
The crocodile is quite fat and stinks
Sometimes he even sinks, when he gets to the bottom
He's totally forgotten
Where in the world he is
But all in all the crocodile's crawl is really the scariest of them all.

William Cooter (9)
Stoke Holy Cross Primary School

SUMMER POEM

I like summer
You can roll around and play.
Summer is cool
Mum can just sunbathe all day.
Summer is funky
Turn up the volume on the CD player.
Summer is groovy
Boys go and meet football players.
Summer is brill
We don't have to go to school.
Summer is excellent
I think summer is extra cool.
There are pretty trees
Summer is good fun
Blowing in the delicate breeze
Summer is the best.

Jodie Finch (8)
Stoke Holy Cross Primary School

PLAYSTATIONS

P   layStations are excellent and good to play on
L   ate at night you are playing until you fall asleep
A   fter playing on it for a long time your eyes hurt
Y   es we have finally got over that level
'S top' says Mum always when you're on a tremendous level
T   he levels last a very long time and seem impossible
A   t exactly three twenty-five children press the green button
T   ime for tea! Oh no!
I   love to play with my PlayStation
O   n every day of the week I am always playing with it
'N o!' Says your brother when you beat him.

James Krumins (9)
Stoke Holy Cross Primary School

A POEM ABOUT CATS AND DOGS

I love dogs
Dogs are cute and sweet and very cuddly too
Some are fat, some are thin.
I love cats and cats love me
Some are black, some are brown, some are white,
Cats are cute and cuddly and very sweet too
Cats can be fat and thin
Cats, dogs are the best.

I love them all loads
Cats, cats, dogs, dogs,
Dogs go woof, woof
Cats go meow, meow,
They are the best pets in the world
And you could have one too
If you could have one, which one would you choose?

Lauren Potter (8)
Stoke Holy Cross Primary School

WEATHER

Weather cold, weather hot,
Weather raining, weather blowing,
Weather good, weather bad,
Weather happy, weather sad,
Weather snowing, weather icy,
Weather cool, weather glad,
Weather thunder, weather bad,
Weather nice, weather not good,
Weather sunnier, weather burning,
Weather bright, weather dark.

Mark Finch (8)
Stoke Holy Cross Primary School

SEA CREATURES

S ea creatures come in all different shapes and sizes
E very sea creature has its own way
A great, white shark is frightening, mean, very vicious and horrible.

C oral sits at the bottom of the ocean just minding its own business,
R eally all of the sea creatures are so different,
E very one of them is different in some kind of way
A dolphin splishes, splashes all day
T urtles swim at the bottom of the ocean,
U rchins crawling across the sea bed,
R azors gliding through the water
E lectric eels glowing in the water,
S ea horses riding through the waves.

Rachael King (8)
Stoke Holy Cross Primary School

THE ALL WRONG EGYPTIANS

The Egyptians built the pyramids five thousand years ago
They put the rocks on logs
So they didn't break clogs but they never ever knew what to do.
They had to pull ten tons so they ate bread and buns
Till the end of the day had come.
They lived in mud houses
And they only wore trousers
And they're always complaining about their backs.

Benjamin Bowler (9)
Stoke Holy Cross Primary School

SWIMMING IS GREAT

S   wimming is great
W hen you are not late
I   am the best but
M y mum is better than the rest
M y dad thinks he is the best but
I   can beat him face to face
N aughty Dennis is my swimming instructor
G ray is here in time for the class he hopes in the next race
                                       he won't come last.

I   n the swimming pool you will find
S   ome things that will refresh your mind.

G eorge is my name and this is what I do
R yan is always going to the loo
E ddie is my friend at swimming
A lastair is always winning
T he thing I do is swim to Timbuktu.

George Kerrison (9)
Stoke Holy Cross Primary School

SPACEMEN

S   tars twinkle in space, it is dark, it may give you a little spark
P   lanets are everywhere, one moon is white,
                              it gives a great fright at night.
A   stronauts fly in spaceships. They like to race,
                              but have to go at a slow pace.
C   raters can be seen on the moon, it looks like it glows
E   lectric wire controls the buggy in space,
                         but they have to remember to tie their lace.

Steven VandenBergh (9)
Stoke Holy Cross Primary School

JACK, MY FRIEND'S DOG

Black and white
But no Dalmatian
It used to scare my sister
A very sad and hectic life that poor doggy has had
But the owners named Oliver, Katie, Sophie, Rosie, Caroline
and Martin
Never get angry or mad
From near Yorkshire to the countryside of Shotesham and one more
step to London
Once every two months he stays for two normal days
In the kitchen of our house, we live in Shotesham
The biggest house in Shotesham
Next door a field thrice as big,
So a place to jump, run and play,
Woof, woof he always used to say.

Benjamin Upton (9)
Stoke Holy Cross Primary School

LITTER

Litter, litter everywhere
There's no time to stand and stare
Pick it up, pick it up
If we work as a team
We can keep the world clean
Mars bar wrappers, Fruit Pastel wrappers
Put them in the bin
Chocolate wrappers, crisp packets on the floor
Some people just don't care
So think before you drop your litter on the floor.

Chloe Fish (9)
Stoke Holy Cross Primary School

THE GHOST TRAIN

Snakes hissing, chains clanking,
Ghosts moaning, skeletons rattling,
Axes swishing as we go past.

Werewolves howling, banshees shrieking,
Vampires sucking, ghouls laughing,
A woman screamed when the dagger came down.

The train clanked on and on
I shrank back as a bullet whizzed past
The train was going towards a mouth
A huge gaping mouth
The sharp, white fangs glittered in the eerie light
We went through the mouth
The train had stopped. It had finished
I sighed with relief and jumped off.

Georgina Ball (10)
Stoke Holy Cross Primary School

JENNY'S MONTHS

January has cold weather.
February brings love.
March is cold and warm.
April bring Easter eggs.
May is fun at the fair.
June is for tennis.
July is my birthday.
August is for a barbecue.
September is my dad's birthday.
October is Hallowe'en.
November is for fireworks.
December for Christmas and we start all over again.

Jenny Wright (8)
Stoke Holy Cross Primary School

HAUNTED HOUSE

As you walk in
Fear crawls up your back
All the rooms are deserted
There's trap doors everywhere
Taps drip and clocks tick
Shadows dance across the walls
It's a spine-chilling place
Where nobody goes
Candles flicker in the old dining room
There's a long blood-red winding staircases
Which lead to mysterious staircases
Which then lead to secret passages
Your hair sticks out on its last ends.
Curtains lash around the window panels
As the wind catches them
Everywhere is covered in cobwebs
There's dust everywhere
The floorboards creak as you walk
There are four-poster beds
In every haunted bedroom
It's a nail-biting place
Hold your breath as you walk
It's all silent
Except from the howling hounds.

Lucy Collins (10)
Stoke Holy Cross Primary School

A BALLAD OF DEATH

There was an unlucky man
Who was stupid enough to explore
A terrible forest of death
With its ferny grass floor.

He walked deeper into the forest
With a happy smile on his face
Then he hears a rattley clatterly sound
Like a wobbly knight with a mace.

He hears footsteps coming towards him
He says 'That sounds very bad!'
Then he sees something in the distance
Which is an axeman who's really mad.

As he ran away fast
The mad axeman threw
An axe at his back
And the pain how it grew.

As he fell to the ground
With a shattering thud
And the axe it was stained
With gallons of blood.

So remember the unlucky man
Who was stupid enough to explore
A terrible forest of death
With its ferny grass floor.

Jake Hagg (10)
Wensum Middle School

WHAT IF . .?

What if my dog gets sold?
What if my dad gets very old?

What if I get in a fight?
What if I get robbed in the middle of the night?

What if I die?
What if my baby brothers cry?

What if I can't go out to play?
What if I can't go out and have a nice day?

What if I won't be able to see my dad?
What if I get very bad?

What if I get bullied?
What if the car breaks down and we get pullied?

Kieran Baker (9)
Wensum Middle School

MY BUM

My bum is as squidgy as jelly,
As big as a football,
It's good for smacking,
And it's good for sitting on.
As soft as a baby wipe,
If I didn't have a bum I wouldn't be able to trump.
You wouldn't be able to go to the toilet
You wouldn't be able to run fast
If I take my clothes off all I would feel is a straight thing
And it would feel weird
When I go to bed it would feel like a straight thing
And I wouldn't be able to feel my bum.

Chloe Palmer (9)
Wensum Middle School

MY EYES

Some eyes are small,
Some eyes are big,
But my eyes are just right for me.

I can see with my eyes,
My eyes are fun,
I can read with my eyes
As if they knew everything.

I close my eyes when I go to sleep
Like a door that has just been locked,
I can make my eyes go cross-eyed
Like a person crossing the road.

I close my eyes and open my eyes when I am blinking
Like somebody jumping up and down on a pogo stick,
I use my eyes for everything.

Some eyes are small,
Some eyes are big,
But what matters is that my eyes are just right for me!

Sacha Francis (9)
Wensum Middle School

TONGUES

Tongues are like Flubber
They help chew Hubba Bubba
They roll into all shapes and sizes
They even help to eat pies
They can fold and even catch a cold
They remember every lie you've ever told
So never tell lies because your tongue will know.

Jordan Butterfant (9)
Wensum Middle School

WHO AM I?

A thin, warm bed ready for someone to snuggle up in.
A cute and quiet bunny rabbit looking for food.
A tiny, golden dove finding its way around.
Midday ready to relax.
A vanilla flower pushing its way out of the bud.
A thin, cold, chip ready to be heated.
A robin waking everyone up.

Amber.

Shayne Pinfold (9)
Wensum Middle School

WHO AM I?

A dolphin bright and busy.
A sizzling egg in the frying pan.
A buzzy bee, buzzing around.
A poppy opening with lots of colours.
A robin looking for food.
A settee waiting for someone to sit on it.
A morning when the bed is warm and cosy.

Mummy.

Natasha Jackson (10)
Wensum Middle School

SNAIL

Greedy snail slithers from predators approaching him
Searching for food, watching one bird which is in the tree
A slimy trail getting longer and longer appears
As the snail slithers over the muddy rocks.

Emma Carr (9)
Wensum Middle School

EYES

Eyes are gungy, gooey and round
You can turn them sideways and upside-down
They move, they groove, they make you see,
If we didn't have them where would we be?
Eyes are like gel squashed together in a ball
Always fat and round but never tall
They can be brown, blue or green
But they're always bright enough to see!

Jade Wright (10)
Wensum Middle School

MOONLIGHT

We know it's night
When we see moonlight
We will go to our beds
Our mum will say sleepy heads
We'll have a nice dream
It will seem
Moonlight will drench the world
Goodnight world.

Rebekah Kendrick (9)
Wensum Middle School

MURDER

There was an old ghost called Otis
He had a license to kill
When he went out into the town,
He loved to make people ill.

He carried his axe everywhere
To slaughter all the people
To celebrate his killings,
He ate lots of syrup and treacle.

Danielle Oakley (10)
Wensum Middle School

IT'S QUIET AROUND MY HOUSE

It's quiet around my house
When my friends are all asleep
They're lying in their beds
And counting out loud sheep.

It's quiet around my house
'Cos the dog's laying on the floor
And only barks when the postman knocks
On my door.

It's quiet around my house
Because someone broke the telly
Mum and Dad are reading
But we don't think it's funny.

It's getting louder around my house
I'm finding more things to do
Dad's still reading and
Mum's playing Elvis too.

It's noisy around my house
We're playing Snap on the floor
We're screaming and we're shouting
Mum and Dad can't take anymore!

Louise Smith (8)
Wensum Middle School

THE OLD MAN

There was an old man
His name was Arthur,
He did have a wife,
Her name was Martha.

She was quite old,
She got very ill,
She stayed in bed
But couldn't keep still.

She closed her eyes and lay quite still,
She grabbed her heart in bed,
Arthur laid beside her,
He cried and shook his head.

He laid about the house,
He wouldn't go outside,
He always sat on the sofa
And cried and cried and cried.

Amber Raven (9)
Wensum Middle School

THE SNAIL

Snail as grey as the oldest stone
When it rains it goes in its shell and curls up in a ball
Its tiny eyes look for food growing in the garden
Then starts moving, tugging its house on its back
Over the twigs and leaves
Leaving its crystal trail
His soft body slips across the garden and gets to his larder.

Matthew Barnes (10)
Wensum Middle School

DOWN BEHIND THE . . .

Down behind the fridge,
I met a dog called Sinead,
She really got on my nerves,
So I threw a hand grenade.

Douglas Sexton (10)
Wensum Middle School

DOWN BEHIND THE . . .

Down behind the dustbin,
I met a dragon called Jin,
He did not like me,
So I stabbed him with a pin.

Ben Sharman (10)
Wensum Middle School

DOWN BEHIND THE . . .

Down behind the cliff
I met a dog called Marc.
We went to the beach,
And got eaten by a shark.

Jamie Rigby (10)
Wensum Middle School

JAZMIN TEAS EATS BEES

Jazmin's knees are being eaten by bees
The kids who are at school start to tease.
Her parents tell her she's got to pay her fees
Her best meal is peas and bees.
One day she was eating peas and bees and just cried
At five o'clock she fell to the floor in pain and died.

Jazmin Wildy & Hayley Ratcliffe (8)
Wensum Middle School

JAZMIN BEEF

A little girl named Jazmin Beef
Had a disgusting habit of picking her teeth
After a couple of weeks
Her gums began to feel a bit weak
The more she fiddled and played about
The weaker they became until they fell out.

Camilla Moore (9)
Wensum Middle School

SOPHIE DOOM HAD A VERY MESSY ROOM

Little Miss Sophie Doom
Had a very messy room
She tripped with a fall
And landed on a ball
The floor was like lead
Her sister cried 'She's dead.'

Rebecca Barnes (8)
Wensum Middle School

THE SEA

The sea,
Trickling slowly through your fingertips,
Like sand.

Going round and round
Like a washing machine
Swishing and swirling.

Sparkling and shimmering
When the sun hits the surface of the sea
Still like the top of a glass of water.

Waves going up
Up
Crashing down.

As rough as a stone,
When it hits your legs
Stinging, sore.

The sea.

Tess Cole (11)
Wensum Middle School

DOWN BEHIND THE CAFÉ

Down behind the café,
I met a rat called Vincent
He did a magic trick,
And disappeared in an instant!

Louise George (10)
Wensum Middle School

DOWN BEHIND . . .

Down behind the computer,
I met a mouse called Pete,
When we went to the fridge,
He went to find some meat.

Down behind the fridge,
I met an animal called Seal,
When he went home for tea,
He had a lovely meal.

Down behind the sandcastle,
I met a dog called Mark,
When he ran in the sea,
He got eaten by a shark.

Down behind the cupboard,
I met a spider called Mick,
When he got his cards out,
He did a good trick!

Lois Tierney (10)
Wensum Middle School

ELLA BARNES

The horrible habit of Ella Barnes
Is that she plays inside dirty farms
She sleeps in hay in the piles
With her homework files
The horse tries to eat the hay
And kicks the girl right away.

Mia Living & Sophie MacRae (8)
Wensum Middle School

SEA SPARKLES LIKE A NIGHT STAR

Sea sparkles like a night star
When it's rough,
It roars like a huge beast,
Then all the sea creatures are ready
For a big feast!
Crashing like a big earthquake
Thumping as a raging bull
Still feels so soft, like sweet sheep's wool
A perfect paradise world
Then you wish you were there forever,
Shining so bright once the sun comes out,
Everyone is swimming together
A strong salty smell reaches its power,
Sounds as loud as when the dragon awakes,
Everything seems to shake
Sea sparkles like a night star . . .

Jessica Canning (10)
Wensum Middle School

NIGHT

Night is a herd of black stallions galloping around the world
She makes me feel like I'm not alone
Her face looks smooth, soft and silky like a kitten,
Her eyes are like fireflies, burning and twisting,
Her mouth smiles with shining perfect teeth,
Her hair is long with wild curls, as wild as a lion's mane
Her clothes are made of stars and sky
When she moves the wind goes wild
When she speaks the Heavens ring
She lives in a mountain of stars with snow and ice,
Night comforts me.

Anita Bull (10)
Wensum Middle School

NIGHT

Night is an ill-tempered brown bear,
He makes me grizzle and groan
His face looks like crinkled and crunched up,
His eyes are like crystal balls.
His mouth is like a slice of melon,
His hair is like flashes of lightning,
His clothes are made of rags and rugs,
When he moves, he moves on his tiptoes
When he speaks he rumbles
He lives in a tree with birds and owls,
Night awakens me.

Amie Bartram (11)
Wensum Middle School

THE HEART

The heart, the heart burning bright
In the body at its height.

Like a cherry lightning up
When its sad it breaks in half
And when it's happy it's full like a cup.

The heart, the heart burning bright
In the body at its height.

A heart is what you need
To live, to think of other people
Your heart, your heart you need it indeed.

Rosanna Feek (9)
Wensum Middle School

THE SEA, AS OLD AS TIME ITSELF

The sea, as old as time itself,
Frothing like overflowing cappuccino,
The touching feel waves give piercing frostbite
As you stand by the shore the silly way the salt spray
Hits you in the face, yet afterwards it stings angrily.
Boats sail across the golden shimmering waters honking their horn
                                                    when in distress,
Angry as Poseidon as the waters roar,
Salt, stones and minerals all the things you find in the sea
Crunching, munching, sweet and sour, no way to describe
                                                    the attacking waves,
The sea, as old as time itself.

Sarah Spooner (11)
Wensum Middle School

NIGHT

Night is a kind whisper
She makes me feel quiet and lonely,
Her face looks like a big marshmallow,
Her eyes are as golden as an eagle's wings,
Her mouth is like a yellow banana,
Her hair is like a golden orange,
Her clothes are made of silk from a silkworm
When she moves a breeze comes past
When she speaks there's a whisper in the distance
She lives in a tree with birds and squirrels
Night sends me to sleep.

Grace Burrows (10)
Wensum Middle School

GRANDAD MOUNTAIN

Mountains are ancient just like your grandad with his walking stick
A mountain reaches up into the clouds like a boy
                              trying to grab hold of a basketball net
A mountains is a sharp chocolate bar with ice cream on the top
Mountains are as jagged as swords broken in half
A mountain peak is as cold as Antarctica
As high as the Empire State Building
Mountains are as stable as a brick house made just that second
A mountain is as green at the bottom as a tropical rainforest
They're just like your grandad because they're billions of years old.

Ryan Wiley (10)
Wensum Middle School

THE PARK AT NIGHT

In the park at night
There is no light
People do not see.
In the park at night
Where there is no light
There is a hidden tree.
In the park at night
Where there is no light
Children do not play.
So the park at night
Where there is no light
Is waiting for the day.

Erin Pooley (8)
Wensum Middle School

STARRY SEA

Sparkling, softly in the moonlit stars
Looking up at the sky, I see
Saturn, Jupiter, Venus and Mars
The stars form the shape of a beautiful tree.
The stars can reflect into the starry still sea
With piers on the bank
So the sea can be seen
The crescent moon shining down peacefully
A halo placed over the creamy white moon
With silver gold plates that look like spoons.
The view is spectacular,
Fireworks can be seen,
Jumping out of the sea,
But the surface is still, like a glass of water.

Nicola Carr (11)
Wensum Middle School

MY EARS

My ears are very small
That's handy as I am not very tall
My ears sit on the side of my head
And get squashed when I am in bed
When they get cold they go bright red
Like a pepper sliced in half.
If they didn't people would think I am dead
That is enough about my ears
If I carry on you will be bored to tears.

Roni Sheppard (9)
Wensum Middle School

CALM AS A SLEEPING BEAST

Calm as a sleeping beast,
So still and silent
But on a windy day,
The calm sleeping beast awakes
Shining brightly as the waves hit against the sand
As the waves hit the sand the sound,
Is as loud as a crashing drum
When you touch it it feels cold and frightful
When you taste it, it tastes like salt
It feels like a scythe slicing through you
But the next day the beast is asleep again
And it's a calm sleeping beast
Yet again.

Joanne Oliver (11)
Wensum Middle School

NIGHT

Night is kind like me,
He makes me feel safe and comfortable,
His face looks blank and silent,
His eyes are blue like the sea,
His mouth is like a silver cloud,
His hair black and blue as the sky,
His clothes are made of mist and cloth,
When he moves it is like a shadow,
When he speaks it's a rumble and tumble,
He lives in a tree with a black bat and a silver owl.
Night is a friend to me.

Daniel Hipperson (11)
Wensum Middle School

NIGHT

Night is a calm and caring person,
She makes me feel safe and secure.
Her face looks like a caring princess soft and gentle,
Her eyes are as round as the moon.
Her mouth speaks softly like the sea,
Her hair is like a soft pillow,
Her clothes are made of soft sand, brown and gold,
She moves like a cloud, smooth and round
She speaks as loudly as the wind.
She lives in a dark forest, alone and scared.
Night is loving me.

Leanne Stubbings (10)
Wensum Middle School

MY TENNIS BALL

It is like a football curving into the net.
It is like a jet flying through the sky.
It is like a miniature version of the Earth spinning around.
It is as green as an unknown planet.
It is like a bird going over seventy miles an hour.
It has an outside like fresh green ivy growing up a wall.
It is like a shining emerald in a treasure chest.
It is like a sphere swerving past an expert player.

William Jones (9)
Wensum Middle School

WHAT IF . . .

What if all my teeth fall out in the night?
What if my best trousers become too tight?

What if I die?
What if I become a man and have to wear a tie?

What if I had no heart?
What if I became a fart?

What if I looked like a cat?
What if I went in a machine and came out rather fat?

What if I get a bad grade at school?
What if I drowned in the swimming pool?

What if I went mad about football?
What if I wake up and was really rather tall?

Chelsea Bales (10)
Wensum Middle School

SEA, SHARP LIKE A SCYTHE

The sea is like a scythe cutting through the wheat.

The sea is like an enraged lion roaring.

The sea is like a mountain full of raging gods.

The sea looks like a clear blue sky.

The sea sounds like some rock music turned up very loud.

Johnathan Yaxley (11)
Wensum Middle School

NIGHT

Night is a world of illusion
He makes me feel unsafe and insecure,
His face looks dangerous and amazing,
His eyes are like glistening stars sparkling in the sky,
His mouth is like a half moon the side,
His hair is wavy like the sea
His clothes are made from the finest silk,
When he moves the ground moves,
When he speaks the world stops,
He lives in a cave with rats and cats
Night enchants me.

Emma-Louise Medler (11)
Wensum Middle School

MY LEGS

Legs can walk, jump, skip, hop.
Can be floppy they can run slowly or fast.

Move and bend, walk sideways like crabs
Shake in the air when I stand on my head.

My legs are hard like a rock
My legs are long like a lamp post.

What would I do without my legs?

Jessica Umney-Kennally (9)
Wensum Middle School

MY PEN

My pen is like a piece of string tying up my stories with its line.

My pen is like a stick lying on my page.

My pen has a sharp pin as its tip, writing on the paper.

My pen is like a flagpole standing up tall.

My pen is like a finger with ink on, writing all my work.

Caitlin Bell (9)
Wensum Middle School

SEA

Like a slippery slide
See the weeds under the sea grab you
It makes me feel warm
It is as still as a stick.
The sea is as hard as a rock
Trickling sounds of the sea spraying
The sea is like a bath with bubbles.

Scott Martin (10)
Wensum Middle School

WOODPECKER

I have a woodpecker in me
It hops and runs
It pecks and soars
It eats and guzzles
It whistles and listens
People want to join in.

Natasha Engledow (8)
Wensum Middle School

MY FEET

Feet are like arms
All strong and stiff.
Feet are like chairs they do a lot of things.
Feet are like a bowl of jelly wibbly and wobbly all over the place
Feet can be funny and not do what you want them to do
Sometimes they do.
Feet are like a seat all shapes and sizes.

What would I do without my feet?
I wouldn't be able to walk
Or walk and talk
Or run and jump
So what would I do with my feet
I could walk and jump and have fun
Or skip and run
Or have nice fun.

Claire Jeffries (9)
Wensum Middle School

THE ANGRY WIND

As smooth and calm as an aquarium
Frothing like a pint of beer
As fierce as an awful blizzard
Crashing and thrashing against the rocks
As warm as a nice hot glass of water
Angry, rampaging like thunder
Shining and sparkling at evening sunset
As furious as an angry business man on a bad day!

Joe Walker (10)
Wensum Middle School

THE OBOE PLAYER

At four thirty, one cold January afternoon,
As we were walking through the park
Our breath hung frozen in the cold air
And the grass sparkled in the frost
We heard some music,
Very mysterious
The haunting song of the oboe player
As the fireball of the sun set and the cold wind blew
We knew something special would happen.

Tim Smith (10)
Wensum Middle School

MY HOLE PUNCHER

My hole puncher
Is a squeaky radio when it is playing badly.
When you push it down
My hole puncher is a hole in the ground.
My hole puncher is as thick as a rubber.
My hole puncher is an animal eating something.
My hole puncher is a squeaky baby crying loudly.

Lisa Holloway (10)
Wensum Middle School

I'M NEVER DOING THAT AGAIN

I once went on a ship
Where I had fish and chips
A storm came,
And nothing's the same
And the ship began to toss.

The ship tossed and turned,
And there's nothing I have learned,
A tidal wave splashed,
And as quick as a flash,
The boat tumbled over.

We went full speed
And caught seaweed,
It was getting dark,
And I saw the park
About a mile away.

Twenty-four hours later,
I saw an alligator,
I was close to the shore,
And the seagulls soar,
All over the place.

Then I went to my den,
And then saw a hen,
I was on the shore,
And banged the door,
And said . . .
'I'm never doing that again!'

Thomas Michael Joy (8)
Woodland View Middle School

SPECTACULAR SPACE

Enormous galaxies,
Millions of bright glowing stars,
The hottest planet, the red, firing Mars,
The coldest planet, the ice, cold Pluto.
The first man to walk on the moon was Neil Armstrong
The two planets with rings around are Uranus and Saturn.
Asteroids float everywhere
Shooting stars, lovely, so bright and so light.
Space is a dangerous place, meteors,
Comets and asteroids as big as New York City.
The spooky black hole will suck you up and spit you out
In a different place.
If an asteroid hits
Boom!

Lee Chamberlin (9)
Woodland View Middle School

MY VOYAGE AROUND THE WORLD

Around the world I have been
Seeing plants and a wolverine
Mysterious things might happen to me
Like being cuddled by a chimpanzee.

Around the world I have been
Camping out in the mountain scene
Mysterious things might happen to me
Like being hit by a coconut tree.

Around the world I have been
Scuba-diving with the Queen
Mysterious things might happen to me
Like being crowned in the sea.

Around the world I have been
Diving deep in a submarine
Mysterious things might happen to me
But now I've got to go home for tea.

Daniel Maidstone (11)
Woodland View Middle School

SPACE

Never-ending vast space,
Dark, gloomy space
Saturn, Jupiter, Mercury, Mars and Pluto are the planets I like.
Dazzling shooting stars,
Black holes everywhere.
The sun is burning hot.
Mars is the hottest planet,
Pluto is the coldest planet,
Mars is closest to the Earth.
Colourful planets
Moon shines like a light bulb
Pluto is farthest away from the sun.
Mercury is the closest to the sun
Milky Way goes round and round and round.
Space is unbelievable!

Eleanor Mills (8)
Woodland View Middle School

SINK DOWN

HMS Unsinkable
Left the American port
To join up with the fleet,
And the submarine.
Once under way,
The crew was busy at their work
After fifty months
Fuel was running low,
The tanker wasn't far away,
To come to its aid.
Nobody knew what happened,
But an SOS was sent,
By the time the lifeboats got there,
Most of them were dead.
All the remaining sailors,
Recovered very well.

Edward Allison (9)
Woodland View Middle School

A JOURNEY TO MARS

I'm blasting off piercing the sky,
As I shoot up into space,
The spaceship is twirling around,
I'm looking forward to being on Mars.

I'm feeling really strange
I'm floating slowly in the air,
I want to see where I am,
I desperately wish that I am with the Earthlings.

I'm getting extremely excited,
I want to see an alien,
When am I going to get there?
Because I am feeling rather sick.

I'm landing on Mars,
The spaceship's door is opening,
I'm getting out onto Mars,
Mars is odd and red.

Adam Stagg (10)
Woodland View Middle School

VOYAGE THROUGH MY BEDROOM

The door won't move
What's in the way?
I manage to squeeze it open with my shoe
Just enough for me to get through
So what's behind the door?
A pile of clothes as tall as me
And they're on the floor
Push the clothes aside with lots of hard work
Oh I found my geography homework
Wade through the . . . the . . . um . . . the pile of things
Did you hear that ominous ping?
Oh here are my new shoes
What's under them?
The carpet, I could have sworn it was blue
Something wet and squidgy squelches through my toes
Don't even want to know
I'm getting very near
Now why did I come over here?

Hannah Davison (11)
Woodland View Middle School

GOING OUT TO SEA

Once I went out to sea
I saw a great huge ship
It was then going out to sea
It was due to leave half an hour ago
He's always late to take it out
One day he'll take it out in time.
Next day a fishing boat came in
It had lots of fish on board
The people got off and took the fish to a fish shop
So I had a whole fish to myself.
Next day I went to a show
And got a front row seat
The actor wore a bow
Then I went to the bar and got a beer
Now the show's over
I race home, climb in through the window.
Next day I jump out of my window.

Bill Grint (8)
Woodland View Middle School

YEAR 3000

We step in the time machine
The floor is gleaming, silver and slippery,
The buttons and gadgets are a wonderful sight
I pressed a button, we swiftly took off
Silently, silently, swiftly, swiftly.

I peer through the window
I see the most amazing sight
Dinosaurs, William Shakespeare
We've come back in time
The kings and queens of different times.

The time machine glides
With a flash and a bang
We stop with a clang
We step out and look around
We're in our home in . . .
    The year 3000!

Charlotte Leeming (10)
Woodland View Middle School

OUT IN SPACE

Space is amazing
It has no oxygen or gravity.
Our galaxy is the Milky Way
Comets, meteors, asteroids and shooting stars
All out there.
It never ends,
It's huge.
Space has a black hole that sucks you in and sends you somewhere else.
Nine planets in our solar system,
The sun and moon give light,
Mars is flaming hot, Pluto freezing cold,
The moon has volcanoes and mountains,
The moon orbits around the Earth.
The Earth orbits the sun
If you're not careful you might get sucked down a black hole.
Are aliens really real?
Space stations, satellites which give signals to us from America
Space is great it never ends.
It's dark and gloomy
Uranus and Saturn have rings round them,
But the other seven planets don't.

Benjamin Cawdron (8)
Woodland View Middle School

SPACE

Space is brilliant with never-ending paths
There are loads and loads of planets
It is shining and dazzling as well
If you are not careful you might fall down a black hole.
You might see some shooting stars, comets, asteroids and meteors
Space can be spooky if you are on your own
There are many different names of planets.
They are all named after Roman gods
From up there you might be able to see that the sun is not a circle
With points coming out
It is a giant burning star.
In space you will find the Milky Way but don't try and eat it.
Space is just so cool.

Hannah Manning (8)
Woodland View Middle School

SPACE

Space is gigantic
Just like Earth
The galaxy has millions of stars.
Space is spooky
Just like spooky rides
You float because there is no gravity.
Space is gloomy
And glows like a torch.
Meteors are dangerous
Asteroids are too
Pluto is the coldest planet
Because it's furthest away from the sun.
My favourite planet is Jupiter because it's the biggest planet
Is there more than one galaxy?

Tom West (8)
Woodland View Middle School

A Voyage Around The World

I've been waiting for this day for ages
Now I am on the ship
The ship is now off to America
We have fifty people on the ship
I am now in the world's biggest hotel
The food was great
We ate like kings
I'm off now
I have to catch a plane to Australia
There goes a kangaroo
We've got to go in that convertible car
We're now going to Sydney
It is two o'clock in the morning
I'm now going to bed!

Ryan Tibbles (8)
Woodland View Middle School

A Voyage To Candy Land

I went to Candy Land
It wasn't bland
For me I say
Hooray.

Where's Willy Wonka and his chocolate factory?
He hasn't gone wacky again has he?
Where's Wigly Wonka and Monka and Lonka
Oh a golden ticket
I'd better nick it!
Oh here he is.

Adam Perry (8)
Woodland View Middle School

A Voyage To Roman Times

I see a boat coming towards me
It had shouting at my friend Lee
The boat was being tossed about like mad
They are getting their shields on shouting bad.
The boat was breaking in half
The Romans fell out
They began to shout
The Romans were shouting at me and Lee.
Killed a Roman with my sword
The Romans getting very near
I am full of fear
I dashed round a corner
Leapt in a bush
They had swords ready to kill me
Lee went out to fight but heard blood sucking noises
I climbed up a tree and laid down
I went to sleep.

Nathan Rowe (9)
Woodland View Middle School

Paradise Voyage

Travelling in the luxury boat,
Slowly gliding through clear, blue water,
And a cocktail by my side.

The boiling sun beaming on my face
Like a fabulous dream,
I could lay forever staring into space.

I really don't want to wake up,
It's like tropical magic,
I'm so relaxed but suddenly I'm cold.

I can hear my mum calling,
I know it wouldn't last,
But tomorrow, hopefully I'll go back again.

Jennifer Crothers (9)
Woodland View Middle School

SPACE

Space is dark and vast,
The stars are made of gas,
There are nine planets in our solar system,
The smallest planet is Pluto,
Two planets have rings around them,
Pluto is the coldest planet,
Mars is the hottest planet,
The closest planet to the sun is Mercury,
The moon orbits the Earth,
The Earth orbits the sun,
The moon has thousands of craters,
Our galaxy is called the Milky Way.
In space there is no oxygen or gravity,
The sun is a giant star.
Neil Armstrong was the first person to walk on the moon.
Space never ends.

Emma Sparks (8)
Woodland View Middle School

SPACE

Travelling up into space
I went with a whoosh.
Stars dazzle brightly and sparkle and shine,
There are nine planets,
Saturn, Jupiter, Uranus,
Mercury, Pluto, Mars,
Venus, Earth and Neptune.
There are two planets with rings round,
Saturn and Uranus.
The biggest planet is Jupiter,
There is the sun, moon, and stars
Space is black, dark, navy, blue,
Space is never-ending.
In space there's no gravity
That's why you can't stand still.
There are black holes
The Milky Way is our solar system,
The sun is the biggest star.
It's in the middle of all the planets.
There is a satellite in space
So we can watch live TV.
Mars is the closest planet to us,
Mercury is the closest planet to the sun,
Space is amazing.

Paige Carrigan (9)
Woodland View Middle School

GOING TO THE RACE

I have been waiting to go to the car race
I cannot wait
Here they come
The cars are going round a snow track
It is going to be great, great, great
I cannot wait.
My favourite I cannot choose
Because I like all of them
To see them race it's great, so great
You definitely need ear plugs
Get ready . . .
Rev your engine . . .
The cars go!
It's superb.

Callum Airdrie (8)
Woodland View Middle School

VOYAGE THROUGH THE WINDOW

Open the window, step into space and be the first to visit Pluto.
Open the window, dive into the ocean and swim with the dolphins.
Open the window, and climb the highest mountain in the world.
Open the window, jump into your body and make yourself sneeze.
Open the window, to find peace and no more wars.
Open the window, to the year 3000, see what the world has become.
Open the window, and jump back into bed!

Scott Guyton (12)
Woodland View Middle School

THE JOURNEY UP THE SLIDE

I really like the look of that slide,
But it's far too high,
But I really want a ride,
Why don't I have a try?

I'll put my foot on this first step,
Oh no my pants feel a bit wet,
On to another I will go,
I think I want to go home.

I'll try not to look round,
I don't seem too high off the ground,
Only a few more steps to go,
I think I'll carry on.

My foot's on the fourth step,
Now my pants are really wet,
Now, I think I'm high off the ground,
But still I won't look around.

My knees are starting to wobble,
I think I'm going to topple,
I've got my balance back,
I think confidence is what I lack.

Just one more step left to go,
Should I go home, oh I don't know,
I'm going to do it,
To the top I'm going to go.

Yippee I've done it,
I'm at the top of the slide,
And it doesn't seem too high,
And I had a good old try.

On my little bum I'll sit,
And go down that silver bit,
I'll give myself a little push,
And I'll go down with a whoosh.

Samantha Parker (11)
Woodland View Middle School

STEAM ENGINE

Flashing breeze you feel
On a big, red steam engine
It smells a bit but I don't mind
I love going on steam engines
They're such fun
Steam engines,
Steam engines,
That's all I think about
I absolutely love steam engines
They are great things,
They might be smelly but I don't mind
Steam engines are lovely things
I don't know why people hate them,
I love them,
Boats, ships, cars, aeroplanes, I like them too but my favourite is . . .
Yes, you've guessed it
A steam engine!

Fern Blundell (8)
Woodland View Middle School

SPACE

I am excited
In my rumbly spaceship
Now let's set off
The ship is ferociously loud
It's better in the sky
Superb in space
I saw all the planets
Saturn,
Mars,
Sun,
Mercury,
Earth,
Pluto,
Jupiter,
Neptune,
Now we have seen all the planets
Let's go home
I would have been worried
If I was lost in space
Near the sun.

Thomas Grint (9)
Woodland View Middle School

SPEEDBOAT RACE

Twirling, whirling here I go
I've got enough petrol more than people imagine,
In a speedboat round and round.

Whizzing there and back
My mouth is watering at the speed,
Good job I packed a snack.

As the finish line
Comes into view
I can hear the crowd starting to cheer.

I've won
The cup is in my hands
It's shining and glimmers the sun.

Hazel Pointer (9)
Woodland View Middle School

THE BATTLE

In my ingenious dream I see Vikings
Rolling in the stormy sea
Vikings all around me in their fascinating wooden boats
Ready for battle
I'm among total strangers
One has fallen overboard
Rough sea, becoming shallow,
Every outsider grabbing their shields,
Their shields as hard as rock
Swords out, hauling boat ashore
Bashing, clashing, fighting
The angry enemy are the Anglo-Saxons
In seconds, the Saxons are dead
The Vikings taking over
Collecting up gold and silver
Pulling the boat carefully into the sea again.
Going back home with everything
Everything they possessed
Struggling against the rough sea
Going home, back home.

Elizabeth Dewsbury (10)
Woodland View Middle School

THE MAGIC TRAIN

I am feeling excited,
I can't wait
This is going to be a special day
We are going on a train
What wonders will we see out of the window?
At last we are on the train
We saw a poor man and an adorable dog
They had scruffy clothes
We had a picnic
A multicoloured pop
We had yummy sandwiches
Then we waited and watched
We got here, we arrived
The train stopped
The train was like a dream
Went to my nanny's home.

Kerry-Louise Locke (10)
Woodland View Middle School

THE ADVENTURE

I'm going on an adventure
Where the sea's the colour of topaz
Clouds don't appear in the sky,
And nobody ever goes.

I'm going on an adventure,
To the enchanted lands,
Where the sand's the colour of the sun,
And feels hot in my hands.

Palm trees the size of houses,
And lots of exotic things,
Where there aren't any baths or taps or beds,
Only birds with the most marvellous wings.

Rosina Webb (11)
Woodland View Middle School

SPACE

Shoot up in a rocket
And see stars sparkling brightly
You can't breath in space
Meteors floating about
Mars is steaming hot
Rocket going round the Earth in orbit
Uranus and Saturn have rings around them
All dark, navy, blue.
Shooting stars everywhere
The biggest planet is Jupiter
There are nine planets Jupiter, Uranus, Venus, Earth, Saturn, Neptune,
Pluto, Mars and Mercury.
Neil Armstrong was the first one to reach the moon in 1969.
Space is dazzling
The sun is very bright
Pluto is the smallest planet
I love space
Space is amazing.

Tanya Sadd (8)
Woodland View Middle School

SPACE

Space is amazing
You can see other colourful planets
But watch out for black holes.
Saturn and Uranus are ringed
Earth spins round
Did you know that in space there are meteors?
There are other galaxies,
There are asteroids,
There are comets,
And now and again there are shooting stars.
Space is huge,
Space is strange,
Space is never-ending,
Space is gloomy,
There are dead stars,
There are nine planets,
In space there is a nebula.

James Beck (8)
Woodland View Middle School

ISN'T IT GREAT

Isn't it great how when you read a book
They leave you totally hooked.
All your troubles seem to dissolve
While the world around you starts to evolve.

Isn't it great how when you dream
No one appears to be mean
A matter of seconds is all they last for
I wish they would last for more.

Isn't it great how when you daydream
All sorts of wonders are seen
You imagine things that no one else could know
The time passes so wonderfully slow.

Isn't it great to let your imagination run wild,
I'm so glad that I'm still a child.

Kimberley Rowe (12)
Woodland View Middle School

THE SOLAR SYSTEM

Tonight's the night I'm venturing where no man's been before
I am going to all the planets there can be, you will see.

First stop I hope Venus
Starting from USA
T-minus 10, 9, 8, 7, 6, 5, 4, 3, 2, 1,
Blast off.
Here I come,
Browney, half white planet
Second planet from the sun
Venus.
No life form there, next planet.
Where next, ah yes Mercury the closest planet to the sun
Could be burning hot, careful.
Still no life hopefully the next red planet Mars
Covered in red dust
Quite near to the asteroids
Ahh, little green people
I will have to go back to Earth.
At last home to the third rock from the sun
Well at least I can say I've been to three planets and
Found lifeforms all in a day.

Gina Atherton (12)
Woodland View Middle School

SPACE ADVENTURE

Space, space a wonderful sight
Rockets flying everywhere
Men floating and seeing dazzling planets
Sparkling stars that look like lemons
The galaxy is a gloomy Milky Way.
The moon comes out,
The moon comes out
So shiny and bright.
The sun appear in the day
If you see a shooting star make a wish.
It would be really nice
If you could go to the moon
Watch out!
Don't fall down a dark, black hole.
Never-ending space
It goes on forever
There are nine planets including Earth
The sparkling Earth brightly shines over me
It's amazing.

Sean Farrow (9)
Woodland View Middle School

MY LITTLE GREEN ALIEN

I have a little alien who lives down the lane,
My little alien is always a pain
He wants to go home straight away
And it's only ten minutes into the day.

I took a day off school to help him get home
After minutes of trying he's starting to moan.
'Get me home, get me home quick
The pollution is starting to make me feel sick!'

'All of the rubbish pouring out of skips,
All of this planet's one big tip
I hate this planet now it's no fun,
I just want to get home to my mum.'

Suddenly we see a gigantic spaceship
'Look there's Mum, Dad, Minni and Pip.'
So goodbye my little green alien,
Goodbye my friend,
Go drive, someone else round the bend!

Jonathan Brockett (11)
Woodland View Middle School

SPACE

As black as coal
Space is extremely amazing
Space glows
Sparkling brightly
Space never ends, it goes on forever
No gravity,
Rockets floating through the air.
There are nine planets
Shooting stars all around
The sun and moon sparkling.
Space is colourful
It's vast
Space is gloomy
It's dazzling.
Black holes
Space is great
There are space stations and space buggies
Pluto is the smallest planet.

Laura Dawson (8)
Woodland View Middle School

PLUTO

5, 4, 3, 2, 1,
Lift off!
I'm jolting like I'm riding
On cobbles
I feel sick
My tummy has weights in it.
The sky's getting blacker,
Bright blue,
Dark blue,
Violet,
Black!
Shining stars
Shining galaxies
Spinning around
The colours are amazing
Suddenly
Crash! A thud!
It's freezing
I've got a tiny spaceship
And there's two spaces in it
My nose is growing icicles on it
I wrap up warm first a scarf then a super coat
With essential heating
I know where I am on Pluto
Twenty thousand million light years away,
I've made my voyage
It's a frozen place,
My mission is to bring back
A piece of rock
It's so windy it's like a
Hurricane, whooshing past,

By now I am hungry,
The food is tablets
I soon get them down me
My journey ended.

Thomas Field (10)
Woodland View Middle School

MY TRIP TO SPACE

Something extremely exciting is going to happen
5, 4, 3, 2, 1, blast off,
I'm floating through the air in a rocket.

We're now going through the Milky Way
Wow! Some shooting stars they're like a lit fire crackling
Brilliant there's Mars
When we sleep we have to be tied down.

'What's over there?'
'It's a spaceship.'
'It's great to be an astronaut.'

I'm hungry now but we have to eat upwards
What are we doing next? I ask myself
We're now going to land,
In the white wavy sea.

The scenery here's brilliant,
Look the white on the waves looks like horses,
Now the crew are really tired
Let's wait until next time when the rockets rewind
I can't wait till next time
I'm going up in space again.

Emmaleigh Webb (9)
Woodland View Middle School

SPACE

Space is gloomy and very dark
Twinkling stars go shooting by
Meteors swish past.
Space is navy, dark and black.
Pluto is the smallest planet.
Sparkling stars look amazing.
Space has no gravity,
Jupiter is the biggest planet.
There are nine planets in our solar system
The moon glows in the dark.
Space contains black holes
Space has no ending.
The sun is boiling hot
Rockets go zooming across
The dark, blue sky.
Space is amazing,
Saturn is my favourite planet.

Hannah Mayes (8)
Woodland View Middle School

THE PLANE AND THE TANKER

The plane has taken off
It's sixty metres high
Everyone has their seatbelts off,
And are enjoying the ride.

The oil tanker has left land,
Sailing on the water,
Everyone is so hungry,
But they're not allowed any food.

The plane's landing,
It's near the end of the ride,
Wait the tanker's right,
Where's the pilot going to land?

The pilot forgot his glasses,
He can't see the tanker,
He's going straight for it
But good for him, he missed.

Peter Berryman (9)
Woodland View Middle School

SUDDENLY TO EGYPT

I can see a dog
It is coming towards me
I'm getting very scared
I don't know what to do
Suddenly I am in Egypt
I don't know what to do
I walk into this church
I don't know what it is called
I fainted on the floor
A man came running up to me
I woke up and screamed
He was behind me
Five Egyptians put me in a boat
Then on the River Nile
I floated away, the boat tossed and turned
I got back home the same day!

Hannah Watson (9)
Woodland View Middle School

SPACE

Take a flight in a satellite
Going up to space
It's a gigantic, infinite, dark space.
The moon glows up above
Black holes have great suction
To pull you into their darkness
There are nine planets in our solar system
Two have rings around their middle.
People go up in space shuttles.
Mars is the closest to Earth
Pluto the furthest away,
Our galaxy is the Milky Way.
Our planets are Mercury, Venus and Mars
Saturn, Uranus and Earth
Then there's Jupiter, Pluto and Neptune
Every planet has a moon of its own
Except for Mercury and Venus.
But don't forget that when you see
A shooting star you must make a wish.

Emma Cooper (8)
Woodland View Middle School

MY DREAM VOYAGE

I hear my teachers voice in the distance
I'm in my fantasy world
Away from school no school
In my dream voyage.

Squidgy, squelchy cars
Wibbly, wobbly jelly
Calm, cool shops
That's my kind of life.

I feel wet and light
It's like walking on ice
Ouch! Ahh! Gulp!
I wonder where I am.

Jake, Jake, Jake!
Sleeping again!
Come on quick
Hurry up Mick.

Laura Parker (9)
Woodland View Middle School

SPACE

Space is huge, gigantic, amazing, magnificent
Millions of stars sparkling away.
There are nine planets
Saturn, Jupiter, Uranus, Mercury,
Pluto, Mars, Venus, Earth and Neptune
Saturn and Uranus have rings around them
All very amazing.
In space it is very, very dark and black
You can't breathe
There is no oxygen in space.
The moon is bright
Space is quite colourful and the planets too
There are mountains on the moon
The smallest planet is Pluto,
Mars is the closest to Earth.
There is no gravity
That's why you can't stand still in space
Space is really amazing!

Abbi Finney (9)
Woodland View Middle School

GLIDING THROUGH THE AIR

It's early in the morning
Before the sun is dawning
The wind is blowing quite light,
I am in a hot air balloon
To my delight.

I think the sun is going to rise
Way up high
Through the skies
I feel quite frightened deep inside
As I see the birds stretch and glide
Now I feel quite a bit better
Then it starts to rain
And every moment I get wetter.

I really love my hot air balloon,
And then kaboom!
I'm all alone in my bed,
Now I know my fantasy world,
Is now only inside my head.

Charlotte Morgan (10)
Woodland View Middle School

RIDING THROUGH A DREAM

Riding on a bike,
Speeding down the road,
Racing other people,
It's like riding through the clouds.

Going through a dream,
It's somewhere I've never been
The moon with craters,
All peaceful and small.

Soft and fluffy are the clouds,
The moon and stars mixed in with night,
Loads of aeroplanes, what a sight
Coming to the end of a cloud.

Going down in a dream,
This is somewhere I have been,
The Earth, with trees and life,
It must be a dream I've won the race.

Emma Johnson (11)
Woodland View Middle School

SPARKLING SPACE

Asteroids whizz through space
Black holes suck things up
Saturn and Uranus have got rings around them.
There's no gravity in space
The sun is dazzling brightly.
The Earth orbits the sun
And the moon orbits the Earth.
There are gloomy mountains on the moon
Mars is red, Neptune is blue
Space is vast.
Mars is the closest to the Earth.
There's no oxygen in space,
There's spooky planets in space,
Our galaxy is called the Milky Way
Mercury is closest to the sun
A comet hits Earth boom!
Space is scary.

Benji Moon (9)
Woodland View Middle School

SPACE

Up in space
There are planets
And loads and loads of stars
It is really dark in space
And a bit spooky
A black hole - I better keep away.
Saturn and Uranus have rings round them
Asteroids are shooting all around.
I'm in the solar system
Space is so vast
Saturn, Jupiter, Uranus,
Mercury, Pluto, Mars
Venus, Neptune and Earth
All the planets.
The Earth orbits the sun.
Suddenly a shooting star
I better make a wish.
We're nearest to Mars
Amazing space!

Emma Wilcock (8)
Woodland View Middle School

THE SPACE RACE TO THE MOON

I see blackened sky
Shining rock on the moon,
Stars as bright as the sun,
The wind whistling through my hair
And all the metallic colours.

Glistening, shining, the most colourful, shivering sight
Coming to my eyes
The dusty round moon,
Rough and jagged
And hundreds of huge round craters.

Whoosh!
I wake up everything's wiped out of my mind,
I can't remember anything at all,
All I can remember is the feeling of reality.

Matthew Plane (9)
Woodland View Middle School

MY WISH

Time travelling
Is what I've always wanted to do
Not in a room
But in a well built, time travelling vehicle.

When I am older,
I would like to invent
A car or a train
Not a bike or a plane.

I would travel back,
To ancient Greece
Or forward in time
To the time when we live on Mars.

I'm not too interested,
In Romans with the slashing of swords,
I would rather the future
When aliens ruled the galaxy.

It's a bit like being a philosopher,
When will the Earth end?
How far does space go?
They are the questions I would like to answer!

Karl Curson (10)
Woodland View Middle School

DARK SPACE

Space is pitch-black,
Comets whizz through the air,
Shooting stars leave a trail,
Space is never-ending
There are nine planets
Saturn, Mars, Jupiter, Uranus, Mercury, Pluto, Venus, Earth and
Neptune
The smallest planet is Pluto,
Stars dazzling in the sky,
Stars burn and make black holes
Our galaxy is the Milky Way.
Neil Armstrong was the first man on the moon in 1969.
Mars is the red planet
Satellites whizz around the Earth.

This is space!

Ben Williams (9)
Woodland View Middle School

DAYDREAM

Daydreams take me on a journey
To a far off place
I seem to float
As if I'm in space.

When I get there
Animals can talk
And pigs can fly
And plants can walk.

Lions are friendly
Horses are fierce
Fish can walk
And rats can kiss.

Someone is trying to wake me
But I can't hear them
I'm in a daydream
And no one can wake me.

Katie Barnes (11)
Woodland View Middle School

OUTER SPACE

5, 4, 3, 2, 1,
Blast-off
Space is vast it never ends,
Dazzling bright because of all the stars.
Earth is the only planet with life so far.
Every planet has a moon of its own,
Except Mercury and Venus,
Saturn is famous for its one hundred and seventy miles per hour winds
All the stars so colourful in space.
Shooting stars fly all around
They form black holes that suck you down
Meteors come out of nowhere,
Looking out of windows space really glows.
If you come to think about it
Space is the most amazing thing,
There's ever been.

Sam Davison (8)
Woodland View Middle School

GLIDING PLANETS

Planets are colourful
Black holes suck you in.
Space is amazing
The moon glows brightly
Some planets are cold, others are hot.
Space goes on forever
Asteroids can destroy planets.
Space can be sparkly
Dazzling stars glitter.
Space has no air
The sun is boiling hot.
Scientists discover new things.
The Milky Way is a bunch of stars
Rockets shoot up
Satellites can send messages.

Nathan Glenton (9)
Woodland View Middle School

ON THE WAY TO ...

Here we go away to London on a magnificent horse
Going through a big field with Kerry
With the wind whistling through our ears
The trees look like they are smudges.

Kerry and I are feeling hungry
We see a green patch of grass
We have a picnic
We jump back onto our horses
And zoom through the forest.

Holly Goodrum (9)
Woodland View Middle School

POETIC VOYAGES

I'm dreaming, dreaming,
Of a hot air balloon
In the clouds
Then above the clouds
Higher, higher in the sky
Higher than birds, aircraft
Then higher, higher
Into space.
I see planets, meteors
Then I see a spaceship
An alien spaceship
Then they take me up
Into their spaceship
Then I woke.

Charlotte Last (10)
Woodland View Middle School

FUTURE FRENZY

F rom the future
U ntold mysteries unfold
T o the future I must go
U nknown places I will explore
R ound the skyscrapers
E very turn a wave off the floor.

F alling, turning, swirling,
R olling all the lights shining
E very turn is monstrous,
N ever deny it
Z oom, whoosh, bash
Y ikes - I'm out of my dream!

Jordan Hare (9)
Woodland View Middle School

SPACE

Space is vast
It never ends
The whole of space is black
There are planets called
Mars, Venus, Neptune
Mercury, Uranus
And lots more
The stars are dazzling brightly
The sun's boiling hot.
There's no gravity in space
So you float around.
There's black holes and you can get sucked up.
Our galaxy is called the Milky Way
There are satellites in orbit.
The moon has mountains on it
Asteroids are big rocks in space.
Mars is nearest to Earth
Uranus and Saturn have rings round them.
Earth is as small as an ant against the sun.
Space is amazing and spooky.

Chelsie Riley (8)
Woodland View Middle School

HOT AIR BALLOON EXPRESS

I'm gliding through the blue lit sky
It's starry and very dark
I can see a circle of dancing birds
It's so peaceful in the sky at night.

I see more and more amazing things
It's like a show to watch
I see the flashing moon
The buzzing bees
What will they think of next?

Down below I see a toy village
Miniature houses, tiny trees, little bushes
The toy village is getting bigger
Oh it's not a toy village anymore.

I come down with a huge bump
I land on my side
I jump out of the big brown basket
I walk home half asleep.

Siobhan Allen (9)
Woodland View Middle School

SPACE

Space is never-ending, huge, gigantic
Asteroids, meteors, comets, shooting past
As fast as E-mail
Jupiter has sixteen moons,
Saturn has eighteen moons,
Earth is tiny compared to Jupiter.
Space is dark, navy blue
There are millions and trillions of stars.
Shooting stars whizzing past.
The moon is bright, shining dazzling
The sun is hotter than fire,
The smallest planet is Pluto,
There is no gravity in space so you float,
There are loads of galaxies in space.
The sun is a giant star
Uranus and Saturn have rings,
Space is enormous,
Rockets blast up faster than lightning.
The closest planet to us is Mars.
Space is *really, really, really* fantastic!

John Taylor (9)
Woodland View Middle School

THE ICE WORLD

I am at my desk,
Learning maths,
When the bell rings in my ear,
As loud as trumpets,
Slowly I walk to the door,
The door to the playground,
Through the door and . . .
I'm in a different place
A place of ice,
I ask myself,
'Where am I?'
I look around,
I am freezing cold,
All I can see,
Is my breath, like clouds,
Coming from underneath the tip of my nose,
And the gleam and glitter,
Coming from the icicles,
All the ice,
Is as shiny as diamonds
And the colour is blue and transparent,
As I slide across the lifted ice,
I feel as if I'm flying,
I slide into another room full of ice
But this room is different,
It has a hole in the floor,
A deep, dark hole,
I walk,
I trip and start to fall,
Fifty,
One hundred thousand feet, it must be,

And then . . .
I land back on my feet,
With the bell ringing in my ear,
As loud as trumpets,
Signalling the end of break.

Luke Goffin (10)
Woodland View Middle School

GLIDING IN A HOT AIR BALLOON

I'm gliding
In the sky
It's peaceful
Very misty
Early in the morning.
I see fluffy, white clouds
Like candyfloss below me.
I can feel the flames
Pushing me up.
Wow!
I look down
I see matchbox cars
And patchwork fields
Lamp posts like lit matches.
I've just seen an arrow of geese going south.
I'm glad I put warm clothes on
It's icy cold.
The flames have come again
I can feel myself going down
Bump!
The basket hits the soggy grass.
I get out of the basket.
I walk home.

Jasmine Palmer (9)
Woodland View Middle School

AROUND THE WORLD

I get on a big ship with my friends Prue, Piper and Phoebe
I'm going to travel around the world
I go to Africa,
Where it's hot.
I go to Australia
Koalas are crawling up trees,
Kangaroos jumping up and down.
America has got lots of famous cities
New York, Washington, San Francisco
I went to France, Paris, Disneyland
I loved it there
Time to go somewhere else
I really liked travelling around the world
It was a bumpy and stormy ride to the North Pole
I saw a polar bear and penguins
Time to go home
In the sea I saw seals,
Dolphins jumping up and down
They look lovely
All the world looked lovely
You should go around the world too!

Evie Warren (9)
Woodland View Middle School

FLOATING IN THE AIR

Today is a special day
A very special day!
I've got butterflies in my stomach
My feet leave the ground
I hear a hissing sound
Will I ever land?

I am excited,
I can see pointed rooftops
I wave at the plastic people
I see dancing flames
Pushing me higher
My feet hit the ground with a bump
I am happy now!

Adam White (10)
Woodland View Middle School

I TRAVEL AROUND THE WORLD

I go on a large ship
All around the universe
First of all I'm going to Ireland
When I get there it's pouring with rain
The rain's all droopy
So I go back on the ship
Off to another country.

This time I'm going to Los Angeles
Oooh I can't wait
When I get there I see famous people
Britney Spears and lots more
I stay there for many days.

Next I go to Africa
Where it is boiling
There are people there
Who I can't understand
I'm tired
And it's a long journey home.
At last I'm home.

Catherine Marsden (8)
Woodland View Middle School

BACK TO THE ROMANS

I was asleep
I was dreaming about Roman times
I woke with a thud
I was in Roman times.
I was in the gladiator crowd
Blood was squirting out
When it was over I was pleased
It was getting dark.
The next day I wasn't in the crowd I was in the arena
I was scared I didn't like it
A man came running up
I remembered in my dream
That I stabbed him.
I hope that I would win
Stabbed him
I got my sword
He hit me
I was OK and then I stabbed him and he died
No one believed it
He was the best in the world.

Deborah Seymour (9)
Woodland View Middle School

NIGHT VOYAGE

I've crossed the tree into the dark woods
Will there be monsters with scary hoods?
Will there be usual animals at night
Or will there be irregulars waiting to fight?

Will this tunnel of trees lead to light
And will it just keep going till I get a fright?
Or will I get a bite
From a tiny little mite?

Maybe I'm just acting thick
But now I'm really sick
Maybe I'm just acting thick
But I'd rather be locked up in the nick.

I wanted to sleep
Without a peep
I wanted my bed
So then I fled.

Matthew Dawson (11)
Woodland View Middle School

SPACE

Up in space
You can see amazing things
Like dazzling bright stars.
Asteroids are huge, hot rocks
Space is black
There are these nine magnificent planets
Saturn, Jupiter,
Uranus, Mercury, Pluto, Mars,
Venus, Earth and Neptune.
All these planets are as colourful as the rainbow
If you wish on a shooting star it might come true.
Astronauts float about when they get onto planets
Saturn and Uranus are ringed.
Mars is the closest planet to us
Pluto is furthest away from the sun.
Neil Armstrong was the first man on the moon in 1969
In the spaceship Apollo II
Satellites circle the Earth
That is space!

Daniel Warr (9)
Woodland View Middle School

THE CAVE OF BAD DREAMS

You get into bed
And close your eyes
And this is the start of the big surprise.
You find yourself at the start
You look behind you, you see a giant
Four-headed, sewage-breath monster.
You start to run
Without thinking
But you're being chased by a monster
You come to a halt to find a loft drop
Still the sewage-breath monster still chasing you
You find bars across the roof,
You start to swing
You get to the end, but you start to slip
You jump, just making it, nearly falling in lava
Running with all your might
You fall into a trap
One hundred four-headed sewage-breath monsters
Bashing out at you and snapping their jaws
You jump down a hole
You wake up
It's only a dream
The next night you go to bed
And close your eyes and this is the start of the big surprise.

Jordan Jones (11)
Woodland View Middle School

ROCKET IN SPACE

The rocket is on a voyage,
Flying through outer space,
Trying to find a new living race,
Its engines roar like a lion proud and strong.

Its distinctive figure soaring through space
Like a racing car in a race
It's as fast as a bullet gliding through the air
As it flies past Saturn and Jupiter.

The rocket roars like an eagle,
As it flies through the stars
And then it nearly crashed on Mars
It soared out of the way just in time.

Like a bird it turns around
To go homeward bound
On its way it flies past planets
And all the stars.

The rocket flies through the Milky Way
It hits a meteorite and gives a sway
It travels on through space
It goes past a UFO and gives a wave.

It lands on Earth with a low gear,
Everyone there gives a cheer
They all have a drink to celebrate
For the rocket has landed.

Adam Loveday (12)
Woodland View Middle School

FLYING LAWNMOWER

I'm on a flying lawnmower,
In the blackness of space.
Whatever happens,
I'll still see the human race.

I'll ride past Mars and Jupiter too.
I can just see Earth.
It's easy to see,
It's green and blue.

I fly past Saturn with its rings.
I see something waving.
It's a little green man,
I think it's amazing.

I leave the solar system,
I start to explore.
I come to a new galaxy,
I'm definitely not going to bore.

I race back to Earth
And I go home.
Then I realise,
I'm alone,
In my bed.

Samuel Kempson (11)
Woodland View Middle School

MY FIRST VOYAGE

Your first voyage is the most peculiar one,
You never mean to go on it,
You can't even say how it happens!

You live in a world of squidgy embankments,
You'd have the time of your life bouncing about,
New snug, warm blankets torn away,
When your voyage begins!

You're sitting there minding your own business when
You're ploughed out of your comfy home
Then suddenly . . .
Bright light,
Cold air,
And big blurry objects making funny noises at you
What's happening?
Everything is new, you no longer feel like you.

But then you're thrust to one of the blurry objects,
It smells nice and you feel at home again,
Is this what it's going to be like forever?

Your first voyage is the most peculiar one,
You never mean to go on it,
You can't even say how it happens.

Jessica Parker (12)
Woodland View Middle School

THE HARD JOURNEY FROM BED TO WARDROBE ON A SCHOOL MORNING

It's so hard to get up in the morning
When the larva bed covers are cuddling you
The luxurious pillow helps you have a pleasant sleep,
You don't want to get out of bed.

The wardrobe is about two metres away,
But it seems like ten.

You stick a foot and a hand out,
But zoom it back in,
It's like the Arctic out there!

You try again; it's so chilly,
But you have to get out,
Or you will miss the bell at school.

You crawl to the edge of the larva bed,
And jump out, run, run to the wardrobe,
Find the school clothes and put them on,
So your fiery hot body warms up the clothes.

Run down the stairs because you smell bacon,
But Mum says
'It's a Saturday.'

Paul Davies (11)
Woodland View Middle School

VOYAGE UNDERWATER

The sea has many secrets
With its trail of exotic creatures,
Dolphins flying as the moon goes by
Whales leaping through the air.

The sea is deep and blue
I swim through its inky depths
And all I can see is a dark black sea
I'm very scared - there's a shark!

My biggest voyage is now to come
As it chases me to the top.
I cannot hide from that terrifying beast -
I guess I'm going to be eaten.

He swims away so he can't be hungry
What a relief to see blue sky
Birds bobbing around on the water
I look around - help! I'm lost!

The sea has many secrets
With its trails of exotic creatures
Dolphins flying as the moon goes by
And me, stuck here forever!

Sarah Loombe (12)
Woodland View Middle School

A LONG, LONG WAY TO THE LOO

I'm in my bed
I need the loo
There's something out to get me.

I cannot go
I am too scared
He'll eat me in one gulp.

I see his shadow
It's very big
I want it to go away.

I'm out my bed
Look round the corner
Oh! It's only my cat Faye.

I'm tinkled out
Faye has gone now
It's a long way back to go.

It's not too far
I can make it
I think I'm nearly there.

I see my bed
I run and jump
I made it, hallelujah.

Tom Robinson (12)
Woodland View Middle School

VOYAGE THROUGH LIFE

In 1988 I had my birth,
And Mum started to tell how much I was worth,
'I would die for this little one
As I would for my only son.'

Then I became a toddler with a pram,
And my obsession was strawberry jam,
Disaster struck when I was four,
And Dad was forced to walk out the door.

When I first started school,
Everyone was like 'Yeah, you rule!'
At first I was scared of the older year sevens,
But then they left, *thank the heavens!*

In my life I will be famous
With twenty-five million people knowing what my name is
The media will want loads of pictures of me,
For America, Russia and the whole world to see!

Then I will eventually turn old,
And the truth of my life will unfold.
Of how I once met Britney Spears,
And was best friends with her for years.

Hopefully this is how my life will be,
With a big house, flash car and me as a celebrity.
But if my life doesn't turn out like this,
It would be life that I would miss.

Tiffany Taylor (12)
Woodland View Middle School

MY VOYAGE THROUGH THE KEYHOLE

Through the keyhole
I can see,
A raging river joining sea to sea.

Through the keyhole
I can sneak,
The highest mountain, every peak.

Through the keyhole
I can spy,
The greatest moonlit starry sky.

Through the keyhole
I can see,
The luscious garden from bush to tree.

Through the keyhole
I can sneak,
A dozy dad, fast asleep.

Through the keyhole
I can spy
A thousand children, eye to eye.

Through the keyhole
I can see,
Anything that inspires me.

Michael Burroughs (11)
Woodland View Middle School

A Voyage Through Dreams

I travelled to a faraway place,
Just me, just I.
I travelled to a faraway place where the stars
Twinkle longingly as though they want
To escape from the large black net
Which holds them back.

I travelled to a faraway place,
Just me, just I.
I travelled to a faraway place where the sea
And the sand glitters brightly
And the sound of the waves lapping
The shore is a permanent harmony.

I travelled to a faraway place,
Just me, just I.
I travelled to a faraway place where the smell
Of coconuts carries on the air
Where volcanoes spout red-hot lava
And the birds sing just for me.

I travelled by day,
I travelled by night,
I travelled to paradise,
I travelled by dreams.

Michelle Jay (12)
Woodland View Middle School

A Voyage Back To Roman Times

I feel my feet on a dusty path
I can't see a thing
I hear cheering fans
I hear a peculiar shout
It is a warrior
He is coming this way
What should I do?
I pull out my sword
I hear clanging swords
I see the Emperor and servants,
Look for their prey.
The warrior tries to stab me
I dash past and stab him from behind
He is wounded
The Emperor turns his thumb down
I close my eyes and it doesn't go through
Now it is time for lions.
I see three huge lions coming towards me
I gasp and run for my life
One of the lions catches me
I cut it and cut it and it died in heap
Everything goes quiet then a loud roar
The people applaud
I am a hero!

Siobhan Ivers (9)
Woodland View Middle School

To Outer Space And Back

When I went on a boat
I went across the sea
It took us to a tunnel
We saw some hieroglyphics
Then in the next minute
We were on land
We got off the boat
We went into a rocket
We were in space
We discovered new planets
Saw aliens too
It was pretty scary
We whizzed back to Earth
We pushed the boat back on the sea
Went through the tunnel
It was raining, pouring, tipping it down
It was freezing cold
It was thundering and the little boat was rocking
We went home to have a rest
And I put on my vest.
I looked at the wall
And it was rather tall
I went to bed
And cuddled my ted.

Gary Davies (9)
Woodland View Middle School

FOOTBALL FUTURE

I went forward in time
I went to explore the football ground
It was huge!
There were millions of seats
World Cup Final, between
England and Poland
I was very excited
It was six p.m. kick-off
There were thirty minutes until kick-off
The players came out of the tunnel walking on to the pitch
The referee came out
Blew his whistle
The players started to play
The noise was fantastic
So was the atmosphere
Roar of noise
An England corner
Beckham had scored
Second half now . . .
England winning 3 - 0
One more goal . . .
Now it's four
Oh no I'm back home
I didn't see the final score!

Aaron Mason (9)
Woodland View Middle School

A DISCOVERY IN EGYPT

I went on a great big plane
To the hot and sunny Egypt
I passed Wales, Ireland and Italy
Which looked beautiful and colourful
After a long and tiring flight
I reached my destination
I took a wide coach to my hotel,
Which was yellow and pyramid shaped
My room was lovely and colourful
Then I unpacked my bags.
I thought it was time for an exciting trip
I got back on the coach
I went to the Valley Of The Kings,
Which was really very small
I thought let's do some digging
I unpacked my long, brown spade
I dug for a short two hours
Then suddenly I felt a step, wow!
I finished all the hard digging,
With help of a few wonderful friends
I tiptoed down the dusty steps,
As quiet as a mouse
I smashed my way through.
A lot of steam lurked out
I walked very slowly inside,
I saw sparkling, wonderful gold
Suddenly I saw a coffin,
Shaped like a pharaoh
I then thought to myself
I've discovered an Egyptian tomb!

Rachel Gaffney (9)
Woodland View Middle School

TRAVEL AROUND THE WORLD

My dad told me we're going on a ship
To travel around the world
It was a magnificent ship
We rush to get going
I'm very surprised
It's great, it's really sunny
I see the blue sea, it's as calm as a rock
Here's an island
It's called Tenerife
It's got loads of mountains
It's getting dark, bedtime
It's been an awful night
The sea tossing us everywhere
Finally morning, we're getting further
It's been three days already
We're in America
It's really sunny in America
People crowded, we travel on
It's been five months
I'm getting a little bored but not much
Here's another country
I don't know what it's called
It's getting misty, I can't see, I'm getting cold
Dad where are we?
We're in the North Pole he shouted out
It's freezing cold, icicles everywhere
It's bedtime again
We're nearly home
What a wonderful time I had
We're home!

Laura Burroughs (9)
Woodland View Middle School

THE RAILWAY

It's just like the flashing breeze
Flashing down grass and trees
Quickly as I dream on
I imagine the Romans came
Came beside the train and then gone!

I wake up with a thump
It's hard to get out
I found a boat and stuck a note
How do I get out?
As it has gone on
I've seen more horrible, terrifying things
Than you have ever seen
Moons and planets surrounded
Jewellery was around me.

You'd think I would take but I didn't
Gold and silver, minerals,
Purple, brown and pink
Glow in dark
Sandy rock, dusty dust.

Swoop of wind over the Mediterranean sea
Cruisers down waves
Crystal glowing, sparkling
Diamonds fluttering
Golden light, flashing
Digging swords, silver
But the sun makes golden breath.

Jennifer Hudson (8)
Woodland View Middle School

THE SEVEN SEAS

I sailed across the seven seas
A storm came and the sea got rough
We got tossed around
Rain ran down our necks.

I sailed the seven seas
I sailed across the seven seas and the sea got rough
We got tossed around
And rain down our necks.

I sailed the seven seas and ate fishy weeds
I sailed the seven seas and the sea got rough
I got tossed around
And rain ran down our necks
I sailed the seven seas
And I found buried treasure in a forest

I sailed the seven seas, I sailed the seven seas
And ate fishy meals
I sailed the seven seas, I sailed across the seven seas
And ate fishy meals and ate fish meals
I sailed the seven seas, I sailed across the seven seas.

I am the captain, I am the captain
And I sailed the seven seas, I sailed across the seven seas
A storm broke out and the sea got rough,
A storm broke out and the sea got rough,
I sailed the seven seas, I sailed the seven seas.
And a storm broke out and a storm broke
The boat sank and was never seen again
So I can't sail the seven seas!

James Chambers (8)
Woodland View Middle School